WORDS OF HOPE FROM HEAVEN

RICHARD LEE

HARVEST HOUSE
PUBLISHERS
Eugene, Oregon 97402

WINDOWS TO THE HEART OF GOD

Eugene, Oregon 97402

Library of Congress Cataloging-in-Publication Data

Lee, Richard, 1946–
Windows to the heart of God / Richard G. Lee.
p. cm.
ISBN 1-56507-501-3 (alk. paper)
1. Meditations. I. Title.
BV4832.2.L415 1996 96-6120
242—dc20 CIP

Printed in the United States of America.

96 97 98 99 00 01 02 03 / CH / 10 9 8 7 6 5 4 3 2 1

Affectionately dedicated to

Dr. William Bryan Lee II
Mary Lee Collins
Elaine Lee Smith

My brother and sisters whose lives
reveal the heart of God
each day.

Contents

Words from Heaven

Back to Atlanta. At last.

Bone-weary after a heavy speaking schedule in a faraway city, I stumbled through the Atlanta airport toward baggage claim for what seemed the ten-millionth time. How many times had I watched those travel-worn bags go round and round on that carousel? Sometimes it felt like a picture of my busy life.

But this was the best part of any trip—coming home.

Anxious to get back to my family, I hurried through the crowds and then out across the parking deck to my car. It seemed as if I couldn't walk fast enough.

Then out of the corner of my eye I caught something that made me pause and forget myself for a moment. On the wall of the parking deck someone had taken time to scribble these words:

I Just Can't Take It Anymore.

Who could have written those words? A man? A woman? Who would have taken time in this busy airport to scrawl his heart on a cement wall? I tried to visualize someone standing there, writing with a black felt-tip pen.

Weeping? Hands shaking? Slump-shouldered? Grim-faced? Washed out and limp?

What kind of person took time to send that message to a thousand anonymous eyes?

Maybe some businessman, overwhelmed with pressures at work.

Maybe a battered and abused wife, heading for a plane . . . and escape.

Maybe a teenager whose parents never took time to understand . . . who in one final futile cry for help wrote on the wall of a parking deck.

I Just Can't Take It Anymore.

Those are words of despair. Discouragement. Fear. Yet such words are not unusual in our world today. The headlines of the daily papers shout them out. The news anchor seems to delight in shocking us: *"Our lead story tonight is one of corruption . . . abuse . . . tragedy."*

E*nough*, I say to all of that! For into this negative, cynical age comes the bright reality of words from Another Place.

Words from heaven.

Words spoken by our loving heavenly Father.

Words of hope.

As the apostle wrote: "Whatever is true, whatever is noble, whatever is right, whatever is pure, whatever is lovely, whatever is admirable—if anything is excellent or praiseworthy—think about such things. . . . *And the God of peace will be with you"* (Philippians 4:8,9, italics mine).

Maybe you saw this book on a shelf or rack somewhere and the title caught your eye. Maybe a friend or neighbor or relative passed it along to you.

However these words came to you, you now hold them in your hands. If you read on, you will hold them in your heart.

And then they will hold you in their strength.

—Richard G. Lee

1

Acceptance
Healing the Wounded Spirit

Rejection devastates.

Sometimes it's like a quick sword thrust through the spirit.

Sometimes it's like a long, gradual slide down a rocky mountainside.

Either way, the pain of rejection can drive one to violent rage . . . or numbing despair. Infants have been known to sicken and even die from lack of attention and affection.

When G. Campbell Morgan, the noted preacher, desired to enter the ministry, he gave a trial sermon in front of a panel of men who were to ordain him. To his amazement and despair, they turned him down for his ordination. Knowing that his father was waiting for him at home in anticipation, Morgan sadly wired his father one word: "REJECTED."

He also wrote in his diary that day, "Everything seems very dark. So still. But He knows best."

Soon after, he received the reply from his father: "REJECTED ON EARTH, BUT ACCEPTED IN HEAVEN. DAD."

Although Morgan went on to be a great preacher, he never forgot that moment of deep pain in his life.

Every one of us has felt such wounds. Perhaps we have endured the disappointment and self-doubt which result from being turned down for a job. Or perhaps we have known the deeper, life-shattering rejection of a spouse or parent. All of us, in one degree or another, know how it feels.

It hurts. Sometimes more deeply than we could ever say.

That's why for 2000 years Paul's words have tasted like cool water in a desert wilderness.

> *He chose us in Him before the foundation of the world . . . having predestined us to adoption as sons by Jesus Christ to Himself, according to the good pleasure of His will, to the praise of the glory of His grace, by which He made us accepted in the Beloved* (Ephesians 1:4-6 NKJV).

Accepted in the Beloved.

Accepted in the infinite love that God holds toward His own Son.

> To know that as believers we are totally accepted by the God of the universe sets so much to rest.

This is such a transforming truth because the real rejection people are trying to soothe is a *spiritual* one. We are all alienated from our God and Creator by our sin. Our broken relationship with Him is the source of every problem in human experience. To know that as believers we are totally accepted by the God of the universe sets so much to rest.

What does it really matter if a mere man rejects us? The One whom we have grieved the deepest, the One who knows the most about us, has accepted us. The awful burden is lifted. We no longer have to strive for an elusive approval that always remains just beyond our grasp. It has already been given, for we are accepted in His beloved Son.

But Paul had more to say on this subject. He told the Romans, "Accept one another, then, just as Christ accepted you, in order to bring praise to God" (Romans 15:7). We are to treat one another as God has treated us. He accepted us freely, despite our sins. In the same way we are to accept each other despite flaws, despite difficulties, despite differences. We can accept one another because we have all been accepted by Him.

Each one of us is unique. We have different personalities, different lifestyles, different quirks, different perspectives, different needs. We don't all enjoy the same food, the same music, the same books, the same people. We even view service to the Lord in different ways. But just like the pieces of a jigsaw puzzle, believers are made to fit together into something bigger and better than we could ever be alone—the church of the Lord Jesus Christ.

In fact, the "uneven edges" allow us to fit together better!

The church is a marvelous mosaic of unique individuals who somehow, by conformity to the master design, lock together to create something beautiful. We dare not reject one another. All of us are necessary to glorify God in this age. We each have our role, but we need everyone else in order to be complete. Imagine the following scene:

The Master Carpenter's tools had called an emergency meeting. Brother Hammer was in charge, but some suggested he leave because he was too hard-nosed and noisy.

"If I'm to leave," he huffed, "then Brother Screw must go too. You know you have to turn him around again and again to get him to accomplish anything."

"If you wish, I'll leave," Brother Screw responded. "But we all know Brother Plane really shouldn't be allowed to stay either. All his work is on the surface. He has no depth."

"Brother Rule is not without fault," added Brother Plane. "He's always measuring others as though he were the only one who's right!"

Brother Rule pointed his finger at Brother Sandpaper: "He's the real problem! He's always rubbing things the wrong way!"

Sounds familiar, doesn't it? You're probably thinking right now of people you know who are just like these tools. How foolish and proud they sound! A critical, rejecting spirit threatens their usefulness.

Then the Master Carpenter entered the workshop to begin His project: a pulpit, of all things! And in order to build it, by the end of the day He had used every one of the tools. He depended on Brother Hammer's driving power to get things started and

Brother Screw's binding strength to hold things together. He called on Brother Plane's level head to keep things in line, Brother Rule's unerring accuracy to keep with the design, and Brother Sandpaper's finely applied touch to assure a beautiful finish.

Without each one of them, the project would not have been completed. In His hand, under His direction, following His design, they worked together in perfect harmony. Each accepting his role, not trying to be other than what they were, not rejecting their place or judging the place of another, they were able to do together what they could not have done separately: fashion an instrument for the spreading of His Word.[1]

Do you know that you are accepted in the Beloved? Have you accepted your place in God's design? Do you affirm the uniqueness of others around you, accepting their differences as necessary to the whole?

There's room in the Master's toolbox for every one of us.

2

Age

Time's Blessings

There is no law in life more natural than the law of aging. The moment we are born we begin our journey into old age. Each day that passes brings us nearer to the end of our lives.

For some people this is a very difficult time to face. One day they awaken to the fact that things have suddenly changed. No longer can they do the little things they used to do. The silver hair begins ever so slowly to fill their heads. Instead of "Mom" and "Dad" the words "Grandmother" and "Granddaddy" have become their titles. Somewhat self-pitied and angry at the world for robbing them of their youth, these people's later years seem to have become a curse instead of the blessing God intended them to be.

But for others it's different. These are the ones who have mastered the art of growing old. For them no time in life could be more glorious. No longer are they caught up in the rat race that pressured them for so many years. No more honking horns and buzzing phones. For once they have time to come aside and enjoy the true pleasures of life.

Remember, some lives are like evening flowers that never really blossom until the evening of life. Seldom do great men of history accomplish their best until after the age of 50. Michelangelo completed his greatest work when he was 87. Verdi wrote the famous "Ave Maria" at age 85. Tennyson completed "Crossing the Bar" at 80, Goethe finished his "Faust" at 82, Kant wrote his best works at 74, and Titian painted his most famous work at 98. Down the list we could go, one after another who achieved their best after their youthful years had passed. With most folks, aging is necessary to give the wisdom, knowledge, and understanding that one must have to make the best of his or her life.

Montapert tells of the day Michelangelo ordered his workmen to pull down the scaffolds, to clear away the plaster, litter, and rubble, and to disclose the finished work of the Sistine Chapel. The crowd stood in awe as they gazed upon the figures of angels and seraphs wrought in the ceiling by this great master of artists. Likewise, one day God will pull down the veiling, disclosing to full view the finished work of Jesus Christ in the lives of people who have been fully yielded to Him.

Look ahead with joy and enthusiasm. Remember Browning's famous words: "Grow old along with me! The best is yet to be. . . ." 'Tis eventide. Better make the best of the light!

3

Answers

Discovering God's Character

Imagine someone tossing a hand grenade at a stained-glass window. One moment you're gazing at the tranquil beauty of some celestial scene, illumined by the fading glory of an afternoon sun. The reds and ambers smolder like a dying fire. The blues shimmer like a deep mountain lake. The greens glow like a spring hillside in the morning sun. It's a scene of breathless beauty and ageless serenity. You can almost hear a faraway choir, faint harmonies carried on a soft wind over the hills.

And then, in a single moment, it all blows apart in a million shards of jagged glass.

It was like that for Job.

In one day, life as he had known it was completely shattered. If Scarlett O'Hara thought the good life was "gone with the wind," Mr. and Mrs. Job faced a killer hurricane.

In a matter of mere minutes, Job's oxen, donkeys, and camels were plundered by raiders.

Nearly all his servants were killed.

Seven thousand of his sheep were burned alive.

All ten of his dearly-loved children perished in a single mighty storm.

A little later Job himself, an honored and esteemed judge, was ravaged by a loathsome disease, reduced to sitting in ashes, scraping his sores with broken pottery.

In his misery he cried out to God, looking for answers: "If I have sinned, what have I done to you, O watcher of men? Why have you made me your target?" (Job 7:20). "Why do you hide your face and consider me your enemy?" (Job 13:24).

Job's self-righteous friends arrived on the scene and tried to help him with his questions and observations, but their answers fell far short of the truth. His tortured conclusion was: "I cry to you, O God, but you don't answer me. . . . You have become cruel toward me" (Job 30:20,21 TLB).

There is nothing more painful to deal with than unexplained suffering. It challenges our faith, snipping away all the clichés and pat answers and leaving us bare.

To question why . . . well, nothing could be more natural.

We live in a world of cause and effect. We expect things to have an explanation, a reason. We want happenings in our lives to be tied up neatly. We don't like loose ends and open questions. But Job teaches us that many times the why's will not be answered. Though he was reeling under the injustices of his experience, Job wasn't told by God what initiated his suffering. He never let Job in on the heavenly conversations that preceded his losses. When God finally did speak to him, it was only to silence Job's mouth with His greatness, His power, His sovereignty.

"You have heard of the perseverance of Job and seen the end intended by the Lord—that the Lord is very compassionate and merciful" (James 5:11 NKJV). God chose not to give him all the why's so that Job could discover something far more important: the intent and the character of God. Job began questioning why; he ended up seeing God as He really is. He confessed, "I have heard of You by the hearing of the ear, but now my eye sees You" (Job 42:5 NKJV).

When that happened, Job was satisfied.

His questioning ended.

The truth of the matter is that human answers can never really satisfy. We don't need all the explanations we think we do. We are God's children, God's creation. He can do with us as He wills. What we really need is to *see Him.* We need a fresh vision of who He is—of His majesty, His sovereignty, and His grace. When we see Him as He is, we realize that He really is all the answer we will ever need.

No chance has brought this ill to me;
'Tis God's sweet will, so let it be;
He seeth what I cannot see.
There is a reason for each pain,
And He will one day make it plain
That earthly loss is heavenly gain.

—Author unknown

4

Never-Failing Power

"Awesome!"

That's what a teenager told me this morning as she described a really neat hat I was wearing while taking my morning jog. I passed her as she waited for the school bus, and with one look at my hat she said, "Mister, that hat is awesome!"

That brought to my mind the words that teenagers have used through the years. How about these:

"Cool, man"
"Far out"
"Groovy"
"Right on"

Remember when those were the catchwords of the day? But now it's *awesome!*

Christian teens even have their own song of faith: "Our God Is an Awesome God." And how right they are! When we consider His nature, His character, His attributes, we are truly awestruck.

First, God is immutable. He is always the same. The writer of Hebrews said, "Jesus Christ is the same yesterday and today and forever" (Hebrews 13:8). Simply put, He does not change. Why not? Because He does not need to change. This sameness means consistent blessings for us all. It means:

His love is always the same.
His mercy is always the same.
His forgiveness is always the same.
His faithfulness is always the same.

Even when we fail Him, He can never fail us. He will not and cannot, because He is immutable and will not change.

Then, God is omnipresent. He is everywhere at the same time. He is both in heaven and on earth. He is at the side of the crib watching over the sleeping baby and beside the soldier in battle at the same moment. Wherever there is a place to be, He is there.

No wonder we can rest in what Jesus told us: "I am with you always, even unto the end of the world" (KJV). Nothing could exist without Him, He is the Creator of all that is, and His presence is the glue that holds everything together.

God is omniscient. He is all-knowing. We need to be reminded of things, but God has never been reminded. We need to be made aware, but God has always been aware. God is not a learner or a student, for all there is to know He already knows and has always known.

That should be of comfort to us. He knows our heartaches, our disappointments, and our cares. He understands because He *knows.*

Finally, God is omnipotent. He is all-powerful. The word "Almighty" is used 56 times in Scripture. Each time it refers to God and means there is nothing He cannot do. The psalmist declares this when he says, "Power belongs to God" (Psalm 62:11 NKJV).

Does that tell us anything about our God? Certainly it does, and the only word I know to describe Him is *awesome!*

5

Beginning

Love Revealed

He was a man overcome with doubts.

He wanted desperately to serve in a certain ministry, but felt it was impossible. He could talk only of the mistakes he had made in years past and the heavy guilt he carried as a result. He really had not done anything for the Lord since. He was a man not only assessed by his past, but *paralyzed* by it.

Tragically, he is not alone in his dilemma. Untold numbers of believers find themselves locked in the same condition: trapped and defeated because they cannot break the fetters of past mistakes.

The disciples could easily have fallen into the same mindset. Everyone knows of Peter's cowardly denial of the Lord in the high priest's courtyard. But Matthew and Mark record the fact that even before this betrayal, when Jesus was arrested in the Garden, *all* the disciples forsook Him and fled. They were all like Peter in that moment. Their failure of faith in a time of crisis began a downward spiral in their hearts. Fearing for their own safety, seeing all their hopes and dreams shut up in a sealed and guarded tomb, they planned to melt back into their former lives and forget they had ever known Him.

And then . . .

Resurrection! At first they didn't believe the stories of the women. They were troubled, filled with doubt. Then, one by one, they recognized Him, fell at His feet, and worshiped Him. He was alive! Hope was reborn!

But what about the past? Would He remember . . . how they had deserted Him . . . how they had cut and run at the moment of danger? How could they have been so faithless and unbelieving?

The past didn't sabotage the present or the future. The disciples' failures would always be a reminder of the weakness of the flesh and the power of sin, but they would not be a barrier to further usefulness.

Never one to upbraid or accuse, Jesus quietly reaffirmed His love for them. He spent time among them on several occasions. He allowed them to touch His hands and His side, to settle their doubts and be convinced of His reality. He helped them in their daily needs, directing them to the location of fish when they had caught nothing and fixing them breakfast on the shore. He opened their eyes to the Scriptures. He gave them the promise of His Spirit, to be with them forever.

And then He gave them a mission.

When they were renewed in faith and secure again in His love, He gave them a charge. Those who had so glaringly failed Him in His moment of trial were entrusted with the greatest work the world would ever know: the spreading of the gospel. The past didn't sabotage the present or the future. Their failures would always be a reminder of the weakness of the flesh and the power of sin, but they would not be a barrier to further usefulness. These men, renewed by love and mercy, went on to turn the world upside down.

The same could be said of David and Paul. Their pasts were marred by adultery, murder, blasphemy, and unspeakable cruelty. If any men should have been paralyzed with guilt, it would have been these two men. But David went on to be called "a man after God's own heart." Paul became the greatest missionary the world has ever known and a pattern for us all to follow (1 Timothy 1:16).

Their mistakes, their failures, and their sins did not disqualify them from following the Lord. They too found a new beginning in the forgiveness and restoration of God.

We all have things in our past that need to be forgotten. There are sins that need to be repented of, confessed, and forsaken. There are bitter memories that need to be forgiven and then laid aside. There are wounds that need to be healed and then remembered no more. We need to "forget those things that are behind" and "reach toward the things that are before."

How is that possible? Jeremiah tells us how: "Through the Lord's mercies we are not consumed, because His compassions fail not. They are new every morning" (Lamentations 3:22,23 NKJV).

Every day, every moment, there is mercy available to us. We can never exhaust the patience and compassion of our God. We may fail miserably, blow it hugely, sin despicably . . . but the Lord has mercy waiting for us. It is never too late . . . the sin is never too big . . . the past is never too painful.

We can always, always have a new beginning with Him.

6

A Shining Light

He lived over 4000 years ago in a region known as Ur of the Chaldeans. In those days it was a wealthy, sophisticated, pagan, urban center, situated southeast of what is now Baghdad.

His name was Abram, but that, like many things in his life, would be changed. Of all the men living on earth at that time, God chose to deliver a clear and unmistakable message to Abram:

> *Leave your country, your people and your father's household and go to the land I will show you. I will make you into a great nation and I will bless you* (Genesis 12:1,2).

Quite a message—especially when we consider that Abram, to whom God gave the new name Abraham, was already an old man when the promise came. At 75 years of age, he and his 65-year-old wife, Sarah, had no children. Yet God promised to give them a son whose offspring would be as numerous as the stars of the sky (Genesis 15:5). For a childless couple past the end of normal childbearing, God's message was astonishing.

At the time of life when most couples would be thinking about retirement, a rocking chair on the porch, and a little peace and quiet, Abraham and Sarah had to contemplate, so to speak, a U-Haul van and new furniture for a nursery.

Abraham was not following a foolish notion or wild dream when he believed he would have a son. He had a sure basis for his faith: God's promise. Simply taking God at His word, Abraham persevered with the assurance that God would do what He said He would do.

Think of it! Abraham had apparently never before heard the voice of this God who called him. He did not have a Bible from which to seek confirmation. There was no Gideon's New Testament in the hotel room at Haran. There were no radio preachers on the FM band. (Or preachers at all—or radios, for that matter.)

All he knew was the voice of God, and stories passed down from the days of Noah.

We have so much more reason to believe God today! He has given us an inerrant revelation of Himself, an actual Book filled with concrete evidence on which we can base our lives. Oh, there are the doubters and the critics who try to argue that the Bible is the mythological stuff of which legends are made. But of course the only rubbish is their twisted opinion. There are literally thousands of proofs of the Bible's authenticity.

Consider the 300 prophecies in the Old Testament about Messiah. Just to scratch the surface:

Hundreds of years before Jesus' birth, His birthplace was named (Micah 5:2).

King Herod's massacre of boy infants was foretold (Jeremiah 31:15).

The escape of Joseph and Mary with the baby Jesus into Egypt was predicted (Hosea 11:1).

Jesus' suffering, death, and burial were accurately described (Isaiah 53:4-12).

His resurrection was proclaimed centuries in advance (Psalm 16:8-11).

The apostle Peter, a firsthand witness to many of these events, contended that these and other fulfilled prophecies are incontrovertible proof that the Bible is true. "We have the word of the prophets made more certain," he wrote, "and you will do well to pay attention to it, as to a light shining in a dark place, until the day dawns and the morning star rises in your hearts" (2 Peter 1:19).

Our faith is not rooted in theory, speculation, or hearsay. It is instead based on *facts*. The fact that God is. The fact that He has created. The fact that He has revealed Himself to man through His written Word, the Bible. The fact that He has spoken as well through His living Word, the Lord Jesus Christ. The fact that every element of His handiwork in creation speaks plainly that He is real. We believe because of *reality*—His undeniable reality.

Did Abraham believe? Of course. Did he ever doubt? Sure he did. Nevertheless, he ranks among the great men of faith, even though his faith was often severely tested. Think of this: Abraham had to wait *25 years* before the promised son was born. By then he was 100 years old and his wife, Sarah, was 90. Yet God superseded the laws of nature to allow the birth of a child to an elderly, barren couple. They named their son Isaac, meaning "laughter," for he brought unspeakable joy to them.

After Isaac had grown into young manhood, the word of God came once again to Abraham. He commanded: "Take your son, your only son, Isaac, whom you love, and go to the region of Moriah." The message continues: "Sacrifice him there as a burnt offering on one of the mountains I will tell you about" (Genesis 22:2).

Still believing, Abraham obeyed the voice of God and took his son on that long, agonizing trip to the bleak slopes of Moriah. Though he did not comprehend God's purpose, Abraham's faith was not shaken. He complied with the instructions, placing his dear son on the altar and raising a knife to plunge into the young man's chest. In the very act of lifting the knife to slay his son, God stopped him. He commanded Abraham to kill instead a ram caught in a nearby bush.

Would Abraham have gone through with it? Would the old man have actually killed his own beloved son? We need not wonder. Hebrews 11:19 provides the answer: "Abraham reasoned that God could raise the dead, and figuratively speaking, he did receive Isaac back from death." Yes, he would have done it, for he was already expecting God to raise his son from death!

Thousands of years, a radically different language, and a totally dissimilar culture separate you from Abraham. In some ways you and Abraham could not be further apart.

Yet in another way . . . you have much in common.

As He spoke to Abraham, so God speaks to you. Not through an audible voice, but through the distinct message of the Scriptures.

As He called Abraham to a life of obedience, so God calls you. His daily desire for you is to obey Him and experience the fullness of His blessing.

As He tested Abraham, so God tests you. Not because He delights in your suffering, but because He knows you will be spiritually refined in the process, as gold in the fire.

As He called Abraham to a life of faith, so God calls you. He knows that nothing is more vital, for without faith it is impossible to please Him.

If you want to meditate on that a bit, just picture an old man with a long beard loading baby furniture into a U-Haul.

7

Changed

The Transformer's Touch

I was recently asked, "What do you think is the greatest evidence that Jesus Christ is real today?" As I pondered the answer I might give this young man, it came somewhat naturally to me: "The greatest evidence is the change in the lives of those that believe."

Although I have studied the many philosophies and religions of man, there is only one that can stand this test: Christianity. Through it thieves, murderers, drunkards, those whose mouths are filled with vile words and hatreds, have been transformed into people of love and understanding. These are the results of those who have been touched by the Master Jesus Christ. I would like to pass these few lines of poetry on to you in hope that you might use them along the way.

'Twas battered and scarred,
and the auctioneer
Thought it scarcely worth his while
to waste much time on the old violin,
But held it up with a smile.
"What am I bid, good folk," he cried,

"Who'll start the bidding for me?
A dollar, a dollar—now two, only two—
Two dollars, and who'll make it three?"

"Three dollars once, three dollars twice,
Going for three"—but no!
From the room far back a gray-haired man
Came forward and picked up the bow.

Then wiping the dust from the old violin,
And tightening up the strings,
He played a melody, pure and sweet,
As sweet as an angel sings.

The music ceased, and the auctioneer
With a voice that was quiet and low,
Said: "What am I bid for the old violin?"
And he held it up with the bow.

"A thousand dollars—and who'll make it two?
Two thousand—and who'll make it three?
Three thousand once, three thousand twice,
And going—and gone," said he.

The people cheered, but some of them cried,
"We do not quite understand—
What changed its worth?" The man replied,
"The touch of the master's hand."

And many a man with life out of tune,
And battered and torn with sin,

Is auctioned cheap to the thoughtless crowd,
Much like the old violin.

A "mess of pottage," a glass of wine,
A game—and he travels on,
He's going once, and going twice,
He's going—and almost gone!

But the Master comes, and the foolish crowd
Never can quite understand
The worth of a soul, and the change that's wrought
By the TOUCH OF THE MASTER'S HAND.

—Myra Brooks Welch

8

Christian

The Heart's Personal Encounter

There are a lot of nice people in the world today who call themselves Christians. Sometime in their past they decided to reform their evil ways and follow the path of goodness and right.

Now this is an admirable thing to do, for the act of becoming a Christian includes this change in one's life, but we must always recognize that Christianity is much more than a mere reformation of the mind. It is the regeneration by the power of God that takes place within the life of a person after he or she has confessed his sin before the Almighty.

Being a Christian isn't just a mental decision that one makes to better himself by the modification of his bad habits, but it is something that God does *in* and *to* a person. Higher than the heavens are above the earth is the regeneration that God brings within one's life compared to the reformed nature a person can bring upon himself.

Christianity is not merely shaking some pastor's hand, nor joining a local church, though these things are good, but it is at its heart *having a personal encounter with Jesus Christ and asking for His forgiveness.* This old hymn says it eloquently:

Rock of Ages, cleft for me,
Let me hide myself in Thee;
Let the water and the blood,
From thy wounded side which flowed,
Be of sin the double cure—
Save from wrath and make me pure.
While I draw this fleeting breath,
When mine eyes are closed in death,
When I rise to worlds unknown,
And behold Thee on Thy throne,
Rock of Ages, cleft for me,
Let me hide myself in Thee.

— Augustus Toplady

John Bunyan said it like this: "The egg's no chick by falling from the hen, nor a man a Christian till he's born again."

9

Clean

Washed by God

William Shakespeare crafted characters and plots that transcend time and culture. The great themes he developed are the stuff of daily struggles: love and betrayal, truth and deceit, innocence and guilt.

His plays live on today because they are as real as the newspaper you read this morning. One of his characters particularly stands out in my mind: Lady Macbeth had her ambitions aroused by a prophecy that her husband would be king. Thinking her Macbeth too soft, she talked him into murdering the noble King Duncan as he slept under their roof. Together they performed the horrible deed, stabbing him and smearing his blood on the drunken guards. Other murders followed as her husband was elevated to the throne.

But the Lady knew no rest.

Night found her sleepless, continually rubbing her hands, trying to remove stains she was sure were still there. But there was no relief. Nothing could sweeten the stench of death she carried. She last appears in the play wandering through the halls of the castle, cursing the spots that were destroying her soul.

What a dramatic picture of sin! The Scriptures speak so often of sin's *uncleanness.* It is an awful stain that permeates every part of our lives. It is an unbearable stench in the nostrils of God. Powerless to rid ourselves of its blemish, we wander through our lives seeking something to wash it away, something to cleanse us of the awful marks of our guilt.

How can we be made clean?

What could possibly wash away the blot from our souls?

The same Scriptures that speak of the horror of our sin tell of a deep, effectual, continuous cleansing available to every person, regardless of his sin. It is found in the blood of the Lord Jesus Christ. Unlike the Old Testament blood of bulls and goats and calves, which could only *cover* sin, His blood actually *cleanses* sin.

The stains of sin are deep. They have seeped far into the living core of our minds and hearts. But Christ's blood reaches them all and removes them. By His one offering He has perfected forever those who come to Him. We are washed from our sins in His own blood. Now we appear before the Father, dressed in the pure and white righteousness of the Lamb of God. Gone are the stains, the blots, the horrible marks of our sin. We have been "washed . . . sanctified . . . justified in the name of the Lord Jesus Christ and by the Spirit of our God" (1 Corinthians 6:11).

We are clean before the Lord.

Clean . . . like morning sunlight on fresh-fallen snow.

Clean . . . like a bubbling spring in the wilderness.

Clean . . . like wind blowing out of the high country.

Clean . . . like starlight in the midnight blue of a summer sky.

But our own hearts whisper a different story, don't they? Living in a world alienated from God and hostile to His grace, we feel the continual tug and pull of sin. It surrounds us on every side. It still strikes a chord within our hearts. And in our walk we still stumble. We still fail. We still sin. We smudge the pure whiteness, blot the clean linen.

How can we enjoy that cleanness of heart and soul we experienced when we first found the Lord? How can we maintain that purity of conscience, that unhindered fellowship? How can a young man—or any man or woman—cleanse his or her way?

By heeding the Word of God.

By allowing God's Word to fashion our steps, dictate our moves, and mold our thinking, we can keep from stumbling.

Just as Christ's blood cleanses from the repulsive defilement of sin, His Word keeps us clean as we pay attention to it and follow its commands.

At the Last Supper, the Lord Jesus wrapped Himself in servant's garments and began the lowliest of tasks—washing the dusty, sweat-stained feet of His disciples. At first Peter protested, insisting he would never allow such a humiliation on the part of his Lord and Master.

You can almost feel a gentle smile in the Lord's reply: "If you've bathed, Peter, you're already clean. You need only wash your feet."

Bathed in the blood, cleansed once for all time by His sacrifice, we are already clean. We need only wash the parts soiled by walking in the world.

That's what the Word does. It points out sin. By abiding in His Word, by allowing it to fashion our steps, dictate our moves, and mold our thinking, we can be kept from stumbling. But when we do stumble, it is a mirror to show us our soiled selves so that we might run to the fountain and be clean again.

"Be humble then before God. But resist the devil and you'll find he'll run away from you. Come close to God and he will come close to you. You are sinners: get your hands clean again. Your loyalty is divided: get your hearts made true once more" (James 4:7,8 PHILLIPS).

The continual application of the Word washes us of the imperfections and failures that cling to us as we go about our lives. *The washing of the water of the Word keeps us clean.*

In our natural state we are no better than Lady Macbeth. We are hopelessly stained by sin. We cannot escape its blemish. We cannot remove its mark. But the Lord Jesus offers us cleansing through His blood and through His Word. He alone enables us to stand before Him as a radiant bride, with not a stain or wrinkle upon us.

Holy and blameless.

Totally spotless.

Clean.

10

Compassion Everlasting

As a mother comforts her child, so will I comfort you" (Isaiah 66:13).

Is any sight more beautiful than that of a mother tenderly cradling her child in her arms, soothing and calming and relieving the distress of her young one?

I remember as a boy the many times my own sweet mother would comfort me. Whether it was a skinned knee from a fall off my bike, a bee sting of summer, or just the tears of a little fellow's disappointment, my mother's kiss would always "make it better."

There is nothing in the world like "mother comfort." And God says this is how He will treat you.

What is it about a mother's love and reassurance that pictures God?

A mother comforts by her actions.

The very hint of a need calls forth all her love and concern. She can pick out her child's cry among the clamor and noise of a dozen others. It's automatic. It just happens. It's part of her nature. The nursing infant stirs and cries:

The mother knows even before the sound reaches her that her child is hungry. When illness or incapacity strikes, her tenderness only increases. She will sit by a bedside or hold the child in her arms until the fever abates, never sleeping, alert to the rustle of the bedcovers, every movement of the limbs. She will spend countless hours helping her child regain lost strength or learn new skills. Weakness, illness, and handicaps only strengthen her willingness and capacity to give.

And so God moves to meet our needs. Before our lips can frame the word "Father," He is reaching out to respond. His compassions are aroused by our helplessness. He comes alongside the brokenhearted and heals the wounded. Smoking flax and bruised reeds receive His special care and attention.

> The Spirit also helps us in our present limitations. For example, we do not know how to pray worthily, but his Spirit within us is actually praying for us in those agonizing longings which cannot find words. He who knows the heart's secrets understands the Spirit's intention as he prays according to God's will for those who love him (Romans 8:26,27 PHILLIPS).

Our weakness calls forth His strength, not His condemnation. Our need will never exhaust His ability or His willingness to supply.

A mother comforts by her words.

The soft answer, the word fitly spoken, are her special province. It is amazing how she can soothe hurt feelings with just a few syllables. Tears are dried and perspective restored by the words of her mouth. But she doesn't merely speak kindness. Often she has to correct in order to properly comfort . . . and she does so gently and lovingly. She also shares encouragement and strength. Hers is a bracing kind of comfort that doesn't weaken through undue sympathy but strengthens through gentle application of the truth.

And so God comforts us through His Word. He speaks tenderly to those who ache. He gives guidance to those without direction. He speaks hope to those who are in despair. His Word is a storehouse of consolation and reassurance. It is also a treasure chest of correction and instruction in righteousness that gives strength and integrity.

A mother comforts by her presence.

Many times not even a word needs to be spoken. Just the touch of her hand or the knowledge that she is there brings all the strength and help we need. Whether it is teaching her child to walk or ride a bike, standing in the wings at the recital or the wedding rehearsal, or waiting in the delivery room for her grandchild's debut, a mother's presence makes all the difference.

It says, "Everything's all right. You're fine. You can do it."

It gives confidence, poise, and strength. Her mere presence seems to bring back all she ever said and did and to seal it for communication to the next generation.

And so God comforts us by His presence. His Spirit dwelling within us is called "the Comforter." He is the *parakletos*, the one called alongside. The Amplified Bible calls Him "Counselor, Helper, Intercessor, Advocate,

Strengthener, and Standby." He is with us forever, recalling to us all that Jesus has taught us and shown us, sealing God's truths to our hearts. His presence is our source of strength, of power for service, of confidence before Him. All that we ever need is ours through Him, and He is always with us.

He longs to comfort you today. Those aren't just nice, religious-sounding words. They are unshakable truth.

If we are not comforted, if we are ever without peace in our troubles, it is not because God has failed to supply. It is only because we don't believe. Our heavenly Father has gone to great lengths to show His heart toward us. There can be no doubt whatsoever that He desires for You to know His encouragement in your anxieties and pains. Won't you turn to Him and receive the peace and consolation He offers you in Himself?

He can be *the God of all comfort* to you, if you will only let Him.

11

Contentment

Surrounded by Living Water

It is a trite saying, but a true one, that the best things in life are free. This is a difficult thing for many people to grasp in this materialistic world in which we live. People think that a new car, a new home, a new dress, or that certain pair of shoes that they've always wanted will bring the happiness they need. However, when they get these things they find they are still unhappy; somehow the pleasures they expected did not come. So they are left bitter at themselves and the world around them, never realizing that the best things in life they already possess.

There is an old proverb of a little fish who overheard one fisherman say to another, "Have you ever stopped to think how necessary water is to life? Without water our earth would dry up. Everything and everybody would die." The little fish swam away horrified, "I must find some water at once! If not, in a few days I'll be dead!" So he went swimming away as fast as he could. But where could he find water? He had never heard of it before.

He asked the other fish in the lake, but they didn't know. Out into the large river he went, but no fish there could tell him where to find water. He kept swimming until he reached the deepest place in the sea. There he found a wise old fish. "Where can I find water?" the little fish asked. The old fish laughed, "Water? Why, you are in it right now! You were in it back home in your own lake. You have never been out of it since the day you were born." So the little fish began his long swim back home, saying, "I had water all the time, and I didn't even know it."

This is like many of us in America today. We have the wealthiest nation in the world, with more things than we can imagine. Yet we still search for happiness from more material things. The apostle Paul tells us, "Be content with such things as ye have" (Hebrews 13:5 KJV). This does not mean we should abandon all desire to better ourselves, but it does mean we should look around and see the good things God has already blessed us with. Contentment is one of life's richest blessings.

12

Decide

Conquering Confusion

It was a beautiful evening as my son and I walked along the beach near Savannah. We pressed our bare feet into the sand and talked about the splendor of the setting sun and the faces which the fluffy clouds painted in the evening sky. Yes, it was indeed a wonderful evening, but amidst all the beauty there seemed to be some confusion in the air. I sensed it, but could not tell what it was.

Then suddenly it came to me: It was the sea. The sea forever tossing and beating itself upon the rocky shoreline. "But why," I asked myself, "why can't the sea be still?" Then I remembered hearing how the sea was the victim of a divided mind, the sun and moon calling it in one direction and the earth's gravity calling it in another. It seems unable to determine its direction—to make a final decision.

I have seen many lives in the very same condition—tossed and troubled because of double-mindedness. The Bible says, "A double-minded man is unstable in all his ways" (James 1:8 KJV). And how easy it is to become double-minded! It is not hard to take the middle-of-the-road approach. It is quite easy to refrain from taking a stand for or against something. Besides, we tell ourselves, it's good to be considered "open-minded." Yet more marriages, homes, and lives have gone down beneath the waves of double-mindedness than any other element.

I remember the story of a soldier in the War between the States. He could not decide which side he wanted to fight for, so he put on the coat of the Confederate Army and the pants of the Union Army. Needless to say, he was shot by both sides! That's the way life is: It demands that we take a stand. We need to settle our minds, to decide once and for all.

Is there some area of indecision that is influencing your life today? Are you, like the ever-tossing sea, being pulled first in one direction and then another? If so, ask for God's help and once and for all determine your direction.

Decide. And when you do, confusion will flee.

13

Everlasting

Victorious Security

Today we are living in the most uncertain society that man has ever known. It is an age of possible nuclear destruction, shaky world affairs, national and local political corruption, an unstable economy, riots, wars, and a host of other negative elements. But amid all the conflict and confusion some things are sure, concrete, and everlasting.

One of our greatest assurances is the Bible's teachings on the eternal existence and supremacy of our God. Among the religions of this world are many gods which one may choose to worship. This has been true from the time of the fall in the Garden of Eden. Many are the cults to which man has turned to try to fill the void in his soul. But only Christianity has a living, sovereign, personal Being for its God. And in our God we can find the much-needed security to face life with a victorious and confident attitude. Our God has always been, is now, and forever will be. In other words, our God is EVERLASTING.

They cannot shell His temple
Nor dynamite His throne;
They cannot bomb His City

Nor rob Him of His own.
They cannot take Him captive
Nor strike Him deaf or blind,
Nor starve Him to surrender
Nor make Him change His mind.
They cannot cause Him panic
Nor cut off His supplies;
They cannot take His kingdom
Nor hurt Him with their lies.
Though all the world be shattered,
His truth remains the same
His righteous laws still potent,
And GOD is still His name.
Though we face war and struggle
And feel their goad and rod,
We know about confusion,

THERE WILL ALWAYS BE OUR GOD.

—Author unknown

14

Faith

Believing Is Seeing

Recently I heard a radio commentator make the statement "Believing is seeing." Of course, at first I thought he had made a blunder and given the statement backward, but the more I began to think about it, the more truth it seemed to possess.

After all, that's the very essence of the statement given in Hebrews: "Faith is the substance of things hoped for, the evidence of things not seen" (Hebrews 11:1 KJV). The very meaning of this Scripture is that through believing we can see.

This reminds me of the story of Bartimaeus. It was a hot and humid day when Jesus came to Jericho. The dusty road which led into the little city was filled to capacity with travelers who had come from far and near to catch a glimpse of the miracle-worker they had heard so much about. The human wall of flesh pushed hard against the Master and His disciples, so much so that it was necessary for them to wedge themselves forward toward the city gates.

Meanwhile in the city, at the place where the beggars gathered to seek charity, sat Bartimaeus—downhearted, dejected, and blind. He was blind to the beauties of this world, for he had never seen the smile of a child, the beauty of daffodils swaying in the wind, or the golden sun setting on the Judean hillside. He was blind—pitifully blind.

But suddenly, as the crowd pushed its way along, he began to hear voices echoing off the mud walls and cobblestone streets: "Jesus is Coming!" "Jesus of Nazareth passes this way!" Bartimaeus knew who Jesus was. He had heard about His miracle-working power. He knew that with just one touch from Jesus' hand he would be able to see. So at the precise moment of opportunity he lunged forward into the crowd and cried, "Jesus, son of David, have mercy on me!" Jesus heard Bartimaeus calling, and suddenly He stopped and asked that he be brought to Him.

"What do you want Me to do for you?" Jesus asked. Bartimaeus replied to the Lord, "That I may receive my sight." Mark 10:52 gives us the conclusion: "Jesus said to him, 'Go your way; your faith has made you well.' And immediately he received his sight and followed Jesus on the road" (NKJV).

Bartimaeus knew what Jesus could do. His request was simple and direct. And the result was nothing short of amazing.

Every great work that has ever been done has first started with an act of simple faith, which might indeed be described as *believing is seeing.*

15

Fearless

Our Trustworthy Protector

Today, perhaps more than at any time in the history of man, people are afraid. Afraid of criticism, afraid of sickness, afraid of losing money, afraid of loneliness. Young people are afraid of getting old, old people are afraid of dying, and on and on with the fears that grip people today. Yet it all seems somewhat pitiful when we think of how God has created us. We were created to have dominion over the world, and yet so many of us are servants to fear.

No doubt this is Satan's greatest weapon to bind, discourage and defeat mankind. When optimism runs high, when success is within a hand's grasp, fear can come and foul up the whole works. E. Stanley Jones said, "Fear is the sand in the machinery of life."

Recently a young man came to me for help. He told me that everything he had ever wanted in his business career was soon to be offered to him, but he was possessed with a multitude of fears that he would not be able to handle the job. Of course I told him the only way to have complete victory over fear is to have total faith in God and in ourselves. But I also suggested three thoughts that might help him overcome his fear. Let me share them with you.

First, we need to realize that many of the things we fear never come to pass. I'm reminded of the famous house in London that the writer Carlyle built. Within its walls was a soundproof room in which the great master would meditate and do his work. Although the house was built to precise specifications for the writer's work, it did have one disadvantage: One of the neighbors had a rooster with the habit of crowing several times in the night and once in the morning. When Carlyle complained to the neighbor about the crowing, the man quickly reminded him that the cock crowed only three times each day and that this could not be so troublesome. "But," replied Carlyle, "if you only knew how I suffer waiting for that cock to crow!" Many are the people whose lives are tormented as moment by moment, day by day, their minds are vexed, waiting for some terrible event that never comes.

Next, we should remember that no matter how long we fret or how much we worry our fears and worries do not help. Nothing is as useless as fear. Someone described the uselessness of fear as "building bridges over rivers you'll never cross."

Finally, the only true cure for fear is complete trust in the care and will of God for our lives. This is among the most difficult of all Christian experiences for us to learn—that God has control over our lives and that we are safe and secure in His hands.

The story is told of a woman whose doctor approached her bed and said, "Lady, we've done all we can; from now on we must just trust in God." "Oh, no," cried the desperate woman, "has it come to that!" To be under the dominion of fear is to doubt God and to sell the Bible short, "for God hath not given us a spirit of fear, but of power and of love and of a sound mind" (2 Timothy 1:7 NKJV).

16

Forgiveness

The Gracious Fountain

There was such a drastic difference
In my uncle and his wife—
Both had weathered years of trouble,
Disappointment and much strife.

My uncle's face was etched with lines,
His eyes and mouth hard-set—
Yet my aunt's small face was soft and sweet,
And welcomed all she met.

"Oh, what's your secret, Auntie?" I asked,
She answered with a grin,
"He buries his hatchets 'handle out'—
I bury mine 'handle in!'"[2]

—Karen Stimer

Unresolved anger is perhaps the deadliest emotion we can experience. We lick our wounds and smack our lips in anticipation of revenge, never realizing we are devouring ourselves by our resentments.

It is not a healthy feast.

Hebrews tells us that bitterness keeps us from experiencing the grace of God. It is poison. And forgiveness is the only antidote.

Joseph knew this well. He had many reasons to be angry and bitter with his brothers. They had robbed him of his father's love and affection. They had taken away his hope by fabricating the story of his death. They had destroyed his colored coat—the hated symbol of his favored place—denying him even a small token of home and family. While he was thirsty and fearful in the pit, they calmly consumed their lunch and discussed their plans. They even profited from their cruelty: Twenty shekels of silver was the final price.

And then came the terrible journey to Egypt. Stifling days stumbling under the desert sun. Awful nights of homesickness and anxiety about the future. The humiliation of being treated as a piece of property instead of a human being.

He had many years to nurse his griefs and feed his grudges. They could have been monstrous by the time his brothers knelt before him during the famine, exposing their vulnerable necks, seeking help from this strange lord of the Egyptians. But somehow Joseph learned the grace of forgiveness through what he suffered. Raising them from their knees, he comforted those who had so spitefully and hatefully mistreated him.

Just as bitterness is an evil root
that can poison and destroy many
people, the sweet, gracious
purpose of God is a fountain
that brings life to all.

"Don't be afraid. Am I in the place of God? You intended to harm me, but God intended it for good to accomplish . . . the saving of many lives" (Genesis 50:19,20).

Joseph's words give us so much wisdom. Anger held *against another human being puts us in the place of God.* Do we really know another enough to judge him adequately? Are we that wise or that free from sin ourselves?

Others may very well intend to hurt us by their words or their actions. We may actually suffer harsh and cruel mistreatment at the hands of family, friends, or perfect strangers, but we have the bedrock assurance that "all things work together for good to them that love God." Just as bitterness is an evil root that can poison and destroy many people, the sweet, gracious purpose of God is a fountain that brings life to all.

The secret to forgiving others is seeing the hand of God in what transpired. God can bring beauty out of the most awful, ugly experiences. His plan is always a good plan, and it encompasses all the evil that our fallen, twisted human natures can throw at it. He is Sovereign! He is Lord of all! Even the wrath of men will praise Him!

Don't be like the uncle in the poem. Don't carry grudges and halfheartedly lay them down, only to jerk them up again when the feeling arises. Bury them deeply, handle down, so they can't be picked up again. Freely, easily, readily, joyfully forgive one another. God is in control.

They may have meant it for evil, but you can know He means it for good in your life.

17

Forgotten

Total Freedom

There is no greater example in history of a man who overcame his past than the life and message of the apostle Paul.

If ever there was a man who had the right to impose persecution, judgment, and bereavement upon himself, it would be this man. Yet from his writings we get this blessed Scripture: "Forgetting those things which are behind and reaching forth to those things which are ahead. . . ." (Philippians 3:13 NKJV).

Most of us find ourselves in the same condition as Paul: We have things in our lives that need to be forgotten. It may be some sorrow, a deep pain, a bitter disappointment, or a sin against our friends or family, but whatever it is, we can take assurance that if we confess our sins to Christ, He will help us overcome them and deliver us from the bondage of the past.

One of the sad facts of the whole situation is that many of us will not allow God to help us.

Recently a man came to me and said he would like to help in the work of the church, but, he quickly added, that was impossible. Continuing, he told me of the mistakes he had made in years past. He had the feeling that if other people found out about them it could cause hard feelings or trouble in the church. Here was a man possessed by his past. He was no good to himself, no good to his church, and little good to those around him.

This man represents a great many people who find themselves in the same condition—trapped and defeated because they have been unable to overcome their past. How much easier it would be for them and for those who surround them if they could come to a real understanding that Christ is willing to forgive them, and help them overcome the difficulties of their past.

I am reminded of the man who applied to a prominent manufacturer for a job. When he did so, he felt bound to tell the prospective employer of an unfortunate chapter in his past. "Never mind," said the manufacturer; "I don't care about the past. As far as we're concerned, your past is forgotten. Now start where you stand." What a wonderful relief that must have been to that man! His mistakes of the past were forgotten! God wants to do the same for us too, but we must be willing to let Him.

The past can only be conquered when we turn it over to Christ. Then we can start where we stand.

Start where you stand—never mind the past;
The past won't help you begin anew.
If you have left it all behind,
Why, that's enough: you're done with it, you're through.
This is another chapter in the book,
This is another race that you have planned.
Don't give past days a backward look—
Start where you stand.

—Author unknown

18

Forward

Courage, Deliverance, Freedom

"The Lord said unto Moses . . . speak unto the children of Israel, that they go forward" (Exodus 14:15 KJV).

The hot and long-fought battle between Pharaoh king of Egypt and the God of Moses had seemed to have reached its closing chapter. Plagues, famine, and death had finally brought the hard-hearted Egyptian leader to his knees. He had released the captive Israelites to go to their God, on to their so-called "Promised Land." It was a painful thing for the great Pharaoh to do, releasing his most outstanding economic resource to march right out of his land. The expert bricklayers, carpenters, pyramid builders, all who were slaves, were now gone!

And it was all because of Moses. Moses had brought to Israel what it had been promised: courage, deliverance, and freedom after all those many years of suffering. It finally seemed that their troubles were all over. But, as is often the case, the Israelites' troubles had just begun. For no sooner did they get out of the Egyptian's sight than once again Pharaoh hardened his heart and gathered his troops together in hot pursuit of the Israelites.

Having reached the edge of the Red Sea, the children of God could hear the rumbling of the Egyptian chariots as they approached through the valley. Suddenly their shouts of joy and victory had turned to fear and bitterness against God and Moses. "Moses, why did you bring us to this?" "It was better for us to serve the Egyptians than to die in the wilderness." The accusations grew and the mob spirit increased as the enemy approached. "Curse you, Moses, you and your big ideas." Then at precisely the right moment, the voice of God thundered forth, "Moses, tell them to go forward!" They must have thought this command to be quite foolish, for they knew that the waters of the Red Sea ran deep and their passage through it might mean certain death. Did not the all-knowing God know this? Yes, God knew their situation, but He knew more, for His knowledge is far above man's. As they set forth to go into the sea the waters rolled back, allowing them to pass upon dry ground. Once again God had made a way.

How easy it is for us to identify with this situation. When everything seems to stand in our way God always says the same: Go forward! But that's the way God must have intended man to be—a forward creature. After all, He gave us two eyes that point forward. He gave us a nose that faces forward, two arms that swing forward from a horizontal axis, and two feet intended to carry us in that direction. Everything that God has ever made is made to go forward. With this thought in mind we should feel confident that no matter what confronts us, we can have the assurance that if we will show the faith to go forward, God will once again make a way.

19

Freedom

God's Declaration of Independence

Not too long ago in the little college town of Fulton, Missouri, the town fathers directed that huge chunks of concrete be hauled onto campus as a backdrop for a historic speech.

They weren't particularly attractive, as chunks of concrete go. In fact, they were pitted, scarred by blows, and smeared with garish graffiti.

But to those who saw them, carefully arranged behind a podium on the broad green campus lawn, they were beautiful.

The speech was by Mikhail Gorbachev, former President of the Soviet Union, in commemoration of another speech by Sir Winston Churchill. In that earlier speech—on the same campus, behind the same podium, nearly 50 years before—Churchill coined the phrase "Iron Curtain" to describe the conditions in Eastern Europe.

Half a century later an ex-Soviet strongman stood at the microphone to talk about freedom . . . against a backdrop of large chunks from a fallen Berlin Wall.

Freedom.

It's become the byword of our times.

In Germany the Berlin Wall is but a pathetic relic of

past aggressions. Its crumblings are now fodder for souvenir shops. The once-mighty Soviet Union is no more, its 12 republics now struggling democracies. Even in Vietnam, formerly vicious Communists have recognized the error of their thinking and are converting to a free-market economy.

What amazing events these are as men seek the higher ground of freedom, of life without oppression.

In the United States, Americans recently celebrated the bicentennial of the Bill of Rights, that remarkable document which has ensured the liberties we have enjoyed for two eventful centuries. This declaration grants to U.S. citizens vital freedoms, regardless of one's race or creed or social status.

It is a marvelous guarantee.

But it isn't the best document.

That distinction belongs to the Bible, God's Word, which details the freedoms we enjoy as His children and citizens of His kingdom. Interestingly, the Bible reveals some fascinating parallels to the liberties guaranteed by America's founding fathers.

Consider the freedoms God has given us.

We have freedom of assembly. Through the blood of Christ, by the new and living way He opened for us, we have the right to assemble with the saints of all the ages before our Sovereign Lord. We have the privilege of continual access to Him. At any moment, in any place, under any circumstance, we can approach His throne and seek His guidance.

We have freedom of speech. We have the liberty to speak before Him whatever is on our minds. We need not fear expressing our doubts, our fears, our anxieties, our angers, and our frustrations before Him. We have been granted the right to be totally open. We have also been given freedom to share His Word with others. In God's kingdom, it is not only the elite who can speak of Him; all citizens may freely disperse His teachings and discuss them with others.

We have the right to keep and bear arms. He has issued to us the most powerful weapon in the universe—His Word. It was given to us to further His cause and advance His kingdom.

> The battle we are fighting is on the spiritual level. The very weapons we use are not human but powerful in God's warfare for the destruction of the enemy's strongholds. Our battle is to break down every deceptive argument and every imposing defense that men erect against the true knowledge of God. We fight to capture every thought until it acknowledges the authority of Christ (2 Corinthians 10:3-5 PHILLIPS).

For the spiritual battle in which we engage, He has also given us the strong armor of His protection.

> Take your stand then with truth as your belt, integrity your breastplate, the gospel of peace firmly on your feet, salvation as your helmet and in your hand the sword of the Spirit, the Word of God. Above all be sure you take faith as your shield, for it can quench every burning missile the enemy hurls at you (Ephesians 6:14-17 PHILLIPS).

We have the benefit of a higher judicial system. Far greater than the United States Supreme Court, this judicial authority protects us and provides us with many rights and privileges. In God's kingdom, His Son is our Advocate before the Judge. He stands in our place, defending us from attacks of hell's chief prosecutor. He applies the price that He Himself paid to every charge brought against us. So complete is His representation of us that we need never appear in court! He handles everything completely.

We have the right to petition. Nothing pleases the heart of our Lord more than that His people come before Him with their needs. No request is too small for Him, no matter how petty. Our petitions are considered precious in His sight, like a refreshing perfume. He delights in hearing and granting them.

Freedom, of course, does not mean life without limits. Rather, it is a life characterized by order and discipline. It may be compared to one who sits down to play a piano. For that person, good music will result only if there is compliance with defined standards. There are certain ways to strike those 88 keys and work those pedals. One cannot simply pound away and expect a sensible result. There are rules and restrictions. But when followed, the outcome can be beautiful. So it is for the citizens of God's kingdom. Only if we comply with what our Lord demands, only if we obey Him, will we experience the joys of true spiritual freedom.

In the famous words of his Gettysburg Address, President Lincoln expressed the hope that "this nation, under God, shall have a new birth of freedom." In the spiritual realm there is a clear parallel to this aspiration. When we by faith receive the Lord Jesus Christ as Savior, we experience the new birth. The life into which we are born in Christ is not without challenge and struggle, but it is the only life which offers eternal, boundless, spiritual freedom.

"Therefore if the Son makes you free, you shall be free indeed" (John 8:36 NKJV).

20

Friend

Love's Liberating Bond

In 1471, two struggling young German artists found themselves in an unbearable situation. Forced by necessity to work for their daily sustenance, the hard labor left them little time to attend art classes or practice their craft. They knew they could not continue in such an arrangement and expect to become the artists they longed to be.

After much thought, one of them made a drastic decision.

Hans offered to drop out of art school and work full-time, supporting Albrecht so that he could concentrate on painting. When Albrecht had graduated and become able to support them through his painting, he would then take his turn. So Hans laid aside his brushes for the tools of a common laborer.

Years passed. Albrecht began to sell his paintings. His reputation spread and he became successful. When it was finally possible for Hans to return to school and study the art his friend had mastered, his hands were no longer able to handle the brushes with the finesse and skill of his younger days. The years of hard labor on behalf of his friend had gnarled and disfigured them.

He would never become the artist he had longed to be.

So Albrecht did the only thing he could to repay his friend. He painted a picture. That painting would immortalize the callous hands that had purchased his fame. Albrecht Dürer's *Praying Hands* stands today as a tribute to the love and devotion of a friend.[3]

A friend is an incredible treasure in this life. Acquaintances abound, and associates come and go, but a true friend remains. The bonds of friendship are among the strongest the human heart can know. Time and distance do not weaken them. They endure, gaining strength and beauty through the years. They are bonds that are forged, like Hans and Albrecht's, in two things: sharing and self-sacrifice.

True friends are practiced in the art of sharing. They have like concerns and interests, similar goals and ideals. They are brought together and remain together because of what they have in common. A true friend knows and loves your heart. You can disclose yourself to him without fear of rejection or ridicule. You feel affection for each other and true loyalty. A friend will be honest with you, even if it hurts. His wounds are faithful, Proverbs says. His counsel strengthens and sweetens your life.

True friends also know what it means to give. Whether it is time or energy or material things, a friend is always giving to meet the needs of the other. We have all had friends who have met us in our times of need: the meals cooked for one another, the helping hand with the auto repairs, the babysitting. This is the business of friendship. Its currency is favors freely given and freely received, borrowing and lending with no accounts kept.

Two Old Testament men stand out among the rest because they illustrate these two aspects of friendship. It was written of Moses that God met with him face-to-face, as a man speaks with his friend. They shared an intimacy, a fellowship, enjoyed by no one else in the camp of Israel. Abraham had been counted righteous when he believed in the promise God gave him for an heir, but it was when he gave up that promised son in obedience to God that he was called the friend of God. His willingness to sacrifice moved God to call him a friend.

On His last night with the disciples, Jesus also spoke of friendship. He predicted His betrayal and Peter's denial, spoke to them of His Father's house, and promised them the Comforter.

Then He began to talk about His relationship with them.

We have been given the incredible opportunity to be friends with the Lord Jesus Himself. To share intimately with Him . . . to enjoy that warmth of heart and openness of soul we have with our earthly friends.

He said He was a vine and they were the branches. They shared life with Him. All they would ever do would flow out of that intimacy with Him. He spoke of His love for them and His desire that they love one another. He said He would soon prove just how much He loved them: He would lay down His life for them.

And then, just in case they missed the point, He said it plainly: "I no longer call you servants, because a servant does not know his master's business. Instead, I have called you friends, for everything that I learned from my Father I have made known to you" (John 15:15).

No longer servants, but friends.

We have been given the incredible opportunity to be friends with the Lord Jesus Himself. To share intimately with Him . . . to enjoy that warmth of heart and openness of soul we have with our earthly friends . . . to know His mind and share in His interests . . . to sacrifice for Him . . . to willingly give of ourselves and all we have for His benefit, for His well-being, for His advancement. He has more than proven Himself a friend to us.

How much of a friend will we be to Him?

21

Gifts

The Unspeakable Sacrifice

"Behold, there came wise men from the east. . . . And when they were come into the house, they saw the young child with Mary his mother, and fell down and worshiped him; and when they had opened their treasures, they presented unto him gifts: gold and frankincense and myrrh" (Matthew 2:1,11 KJV).

There are many wonderful seasons of the year, but none is more special than Christmas. Somehow this seems to be the center of the year, for this is the time to celebrate the birth of our Lord. It has been the custom of our family on Christmas Eve to bake a cake and have a party for Baby Jesus. We gather around the table and read Luke's account of Jesus' birth. Then we pray together and thank God for giving us His Son.

Of course, to children (and to me also!) there is another wonderful time—Christmas morning. As little hands tear open packages the room is filled with shrills of joy. What a wonderful time it is to enjoy the gifts that are exchanged. They remind me of the first gifts that were given in celebration of Jesus' birth. The Bible says that wise men, guided by a star, came to the little town of Bethlehem to pay tribute to the child Jesus, bringing with them presents of gold, frankincense, and myrrh. Strange gifts for a child, we might think, but not so strange after further thought.

The first gift was gold—the metal of deity, the metal of kings. Truly this was a significant gift to the King of kings. Never had the world seen a king like this one. David had come and gone. Solomon's kingdom with all its wealth and power had passed away. Every kingdom that has risen throughout history has fallen except one—the kingdom born to Bethlehem. As the Bible puts it, "Of his kingdom there shall be no end."

The second gift was frankincense—the fragrant resin that has been used both as a medicine and as incense on the altar of God. The prophet Isaiah spoke of Jesus as the One who would suffer stripes on His back that men might be healed. There is no greater medicine for the soul, mind, or body than the medicine that Jesus gives.

The last gift was myrrh—the embalming spice that Nicodemus and Joseph of Arimathea used when they took Jesus from the cross after His death (John 19:39). This symbolized the reason Christ was born: that He might die for the sins of us all, becoming our Great High Priest, our living King of kings and Lord of lords. Thanks be unto God for His unspeakable gift!

22

Giving

Offering Bountiful Resources

There are two seas in the Holy Land. The northern sea, called the Sea of Galilee, is one of the land's most beautiful features. Fed by the Jordan River, it waters fertile valleys and helps produce a bounty of fruits and vegetables. Fishermen still ply its depths, finding sustenance and profit.

This is the sea that Jesus loved. He knew its waters in stillness and in storm. Upon its banks He taught many parables, spent many nights, and worked His miracles of love and compassion.

The southern sea, further down the Jordan River, differs greatly from the Sea of Galilee. Its air is filled with the stench of debris and filth. No man or beast will drink from its sour waters. No children play along its polluted shores, for this is a lifeless sea. Its very name reveals its nature: the Dead Sea.

Both seas are fed by the same river. So why the stark difference? Simply because the Dead Sea has an inlet to receive the fresh waters, but no outlet to send them on. The fresh waters pour in, only to stagnate and decay.

I have known people like this, people whose lives smell of greed and selfishness. They are takers, hoarders, accumulators, interested only in gaining and reserving more and more for themselves. Their eyes constantly on the "bottom line," they do not seem to sense themselves sinking deeper and deeper into their self-made sea of deadness. They are like the man in the parable who sought to build bigger barns to protect his increase, never realizing the true nature of life and riches.

But then I've also known people like the Sea of Galilee, people who receive freely and give freely.

Such a man was the great industrialist R. G. LeTourneau. My father, Bill Lee, was Mr. LeTourneau's office manager and personal friend for many years. LeTourneau was many times over a millionaire, but gave *90 percent* of his earnings to the cause of Christ. As a child I would often hear him say, "Friends, you just can't outgive God." His life was full and rich and productive because he had learned the secret of giving and receiving.

Another such man was George Mueller of Bristol, England.

In the 1800s, Mueller became deeply concerned about the needs of children in his community. He felt God leading him to establish a day school and an orphanage to care for them. He determined to not ask for the funds either to begin or maintain the work, believing that his heavenly Father would both know and provide as He saw fit. The first offering he received was a few shillings. But over the course of some 63 years of his stewardship, Mueller's journals reveal an astonishing account of God's supply.

As a result of prayer alone, nearly 40 million pounds were donated to his ministries. That totals more than one billion dollars in today's currencies! But that's not the real story. The real story is the giving. Out of those offerings George Mueller not only cared for over 2,000 orphans in his five homes, but he also provided day-school education for 121,000 pupils; distributed nearly 300,000 Bibles, 1.5 million New Testaments, and 111 million tracts; and supported several hundred missionaries. His personal giving amounted to over 2 million pounds in his lifetime. Yet when he died, his personal estate was valued at the equivalent of only 850 dollars (with over half of the amount in household effects and personal items).

It would have been very easy for Mueller to have developed into a "taker," but instead he chose the joy of giving.

He wrote, *"The Lord pours in while we seek to pour out."*

George Mueller had discovered "Galilee living." God was free to use him to meet the needs of incredible numbers of people because he never saw what was given as his to do with as he pleased. Everything was God's, and he was but a steward with the responsibility of passing it on in whatever manner God wished. Content to live totally dependent upon God's supply, Mueller also experienced the joy of sharing that supply with others, knowing he was losing nothing in the giving.

Both George Mueller and R. G. LeTourneau lived the truth of Proverbs 11:25: "A generous man will prosper; he who refreshes others will himself be refreshed."

The Sea of Galilee. The Dead Sea.

A freshwater lake teeming with life. A sinkhole with the smell of death.

It's more than a geography lesson—it's a portrait of our lives . . . one way or the other.

23

Good

We Have a Choice

"*Be not overcome of evil, but overcome evil with good*" (Romans 12:21 KJV).

Most people have enemies, and the reasons for this may be many. Someone may not like us for the way we believe or stand on certain issues. Someone may become our enemy because of jealousy or envy for some of the blessings that God has given us. Others may not care for us because of something we unknowingly said or did, and someone else may just not "like our looks." One of life's greatest accomplishments is the art of dealing with our enemies in the way that God would have us to.

Within the Bible we see two ways of dealing with our enemies. They are simply the right way and the wrong way. Let us first consider the wrong way, the method that Haman the Amalekite used against Mordecai the Jew. Then let us consider the right way, the way of Joseph with his evil brothers.

In the book of Esther we find the story of Haman and Mordecai. To be brief, Haman was given the ring from the finger of the King of Persia. In all the world there was no greater symbol of strength than the ring of this king. The man who wore this ring carried with him the greatest respect and honor of the kingdom, and anything he desired was his. Haman was the King's man, and as he rode through the city gates everyone would bow to the ground in showing him respect. Everyone, that is, except a Jew named Mordecai. Mordecai knew that Haman was a wicked man, and he had determined in his heart to show him no honor by bowing before him. What hatred would spring up in Haman's heart as he would pass through the city gates with everyone bowing but that little Jew! The more he thought of it, the more he was possessed with an insane hatred and wild thirst for vengeance. Never had a man planned such a terrible revenge, for Haman planned not only the death of Mordecai, but of the entire Jewish race as well. Later we read the results of Haman's wicked plan: "They hanged Haman on the gallows he had prepared for Mordecai" (Esther 7:10).

Haman was a victim of his own hate, hanged on the gallows he had prepared for another person. He had the entire Persian Empire at his feet, and all the known world was his, but when he saw a solitary Jew who would not bow, that spoiled it all!

Is this not the story of many lives—letting hatred linger within our mind until it destroys all that we have or ever hope to have? Hatred is the one sin within the human heart that carries with it all crime and wickedness. Perhaps this is why Christ said, "Whosoever is angry with his brother without a cause shall be in danger of the judgment" (Matthew 5:22 KJV). The life and death of Haman is a good example of what happens to someone who tries to overcome his enemies by hatred and vengeance. It is the wrong way.

Now consider the right way. The Bible says, "Be not overcome of evil, but overcome evil with good." This is a difficult Scripture for us to understand—doing good to those who wrong us. When we have our feelings hurt, we don't feel like doing good. When someone has told an untruth about us, when someone has stolen from us, or when for a thousand other reasons we feel like lashing back, we are faced with the Scripture: Overcome evil with good.

As we look at the story of Joseph, we better understand this command. Joseph was stripped and beaten, sold into Egyptian bondage by his own brothers, and falsely accused of a hideous crime. Then he found himself in the depths of a cold prison cell. How easy it would have been for him to hate! On the cold dark days, how human it would have been for him to swear vengeance upon his brothers! But he didn't, and through a miracle of God he later found himself a ruler in Egypt.

Later in Joseph's life we see his brothers coming to him to beg food for their famined country. He easily could have killed them or cast them into prison, but instead he forgave them, fed them, and took them in. The Bible says, "If thine enemy hunger, feed him; if he thirst, give him drink; for in so doing thou shalt heap coals of fire on his head" (Romans 12:20 KJV). We have a choice: We can treat our enemies like Haman did and hang on our own gallows, or we can show the love of Joseph.

Evil can indeed be overcome with good!

24

Grace

From Predator to Preacher

He had quite a reputation among the elders.

He was fast becoming their champion, the defender of all that was right and pure in their faith. He burned with a holy fire against the ever-growing heresy that threatened their traditions. With fierce energy he pursued the upstart's followers, mercilessly forcing them to blaspheme the Name they revered. Many of them he threw into prison, casting his vote in favor of their deaths.

But a blinding light on the road and a voice from heaven changed this man's life forever. At the height of his glory, at the apex of his career, he came face-to-face with the One he was trying to destroy. God's grace interrupted his life and he was never the same again. The fanatical messenger Saul became the devoted apostle Paul, the vessel through whom God would reveal the greatest New Testament truths to His church.

No other biblical writer speaks so often of the grace of God. Paul revealed grace as the source of salvation, bringing redemption, justification, and the forgiveness of sin.

Paul knew well what it meant to be forgiven.

Like a first-century Gestapo officer, his hands had

snatched mothers and fathers away from screaming children, hauling them to prison.

His ears had heard their tortured confessions of blasphemy. He had looked into their faces as they died for the faith he now embraced.

But for the grace of God, Paul could have been a haunted man. That is why his words to the Ephesians ring with such power: "In him we have redemption through his blood, the forgiveness of sins, in accordance with the riches of God's grace that he lavished on us with all wisdom and understanding" (Ephesians 1:7,8).

Paul came to know God's grace in another dimension as well. Gloriously set free from sin, powerfully ministering the faith he once despised, the great apostle found himself suddenly hindered. Something arose in his life that caused him pain and torment.

It harassed him, beat upon him, weakened him just when he needed to be strong. So he prayed. Not once, not twice, but three times he pled with God to remove the irritant. God's answer rings through the ages:

> My grace is sufficient for you, for my power is made perfect in weakness (2 Corinthians 12:9).

Paul had long known the power of God's grace for his sin. Now he would discover the power of God's grace for his weakness.

Sufficient grace—enough to meet any need that arises. That is the promise. As Paul penned to the Corinthians:

> God is able to make all grace abound to you, so that in all things at all times, having all that

> you need, you will abound in every good work (2 Corinthians 9:8).

Peter speaks in his epistle's first chapter of the many trials that we may face. He calls them "manifold temptations." The word really means "many-colored." There are so many different kinds of hurts and difficulties in the world. We might be gripped by some physical illness or pain. We might suffer financial pressures or loss. We might face a slashing attack against our name and reputation. We might experience the emotional pain of a wayward child or the death of a loved one. No one's trial is exactly like anyone else's. Each is unique. Each comes in a slightly different shade.

Then, in the fourth chapter, Peter uses the same word "manifold" to speak of something else: *the grace of God.* God's grace also comes in every hue and every color! Whatever the need, whatever the weakness, whatever the tint or hue of your sorrow or difficulty, there is *corresponding grace to match it!*

Multicolored trials. Multicolored grace.

He has grace for every trial, strength for every weakness, joy for every sorrow.

And He never runs out! He always has more than enough.

His grace is great enough to meet the great things,
The crashing waves that overwhelm the soul,
The roaring winds that leave us stunned and breathless,
The sudden storms beyond our life's control.
His grace is great enough to meet the small things,
The little pin-prick troubles that annoy,
The insect worries, buzzing and persistent,
The squeaking wheels that grate upon our joy.[4]

What was it, Paul, that met you on the road that day and changed your life forever?

What was it that transformed you from predator of the faithful to preacher of the faith?

What was it that took your weaknesses and made them showcases of God's strength and power?

It was grace.

Ever and always—amazing, amazing grace.

25

Grouchitis

The Ancient Cure

Have you ever known someone who had the disease of Grouchitis? I have. Grouchitis is a psychological disease that seems to infect us all at times, but for some people it is a chronic situation that never seems to end. Its symptoms are easily recognizable: a frowning face, a fault-finding spirit, an everybody-is-wrong-and-I-am-right attitude, and an occasional "Well, who do they think they are?" comment. All of these point to a clear case of grouchitis infection.

I recently had dinner with a close personal friend. It seems that he was the possessor of just such a problem. Throughout the meal he told me what was wrong with his world, his church, his family, and his friends. When he asked for my advice as a minister, he seemed quite shocked when I showed him his troubles were caused by his sour attitude, which I diagnosed as chronic Grouchitis. Upon realizing his problem he thanked me and left with a new determination in his heart to make a new start, beginning with himself.

My father once told me the story of a young pastor who was desperately trying to finish preparing his Sunday sermon on Saturday night. Each time he would reach some crucial point his little boy would come, knock on his office door, and disturb him. He would have loved to play with the little lad, but time was of utmost importance and he had to continue his work. Finally, after several more interruptions, the young pastor picked up a magazine, thumbed through it, and tore out a map of the world. As he cut the map into a puzzle he said, "Here, Son, take this puzzle out and put it together, and when you're finished Daddy will play with you."

Such an impossible task, he thought, for such a little boy. A few minutes passed and once again the knock came at the office door. Opening the door, he was startled to see that the little fellow had put the difficult map back together in perfect order. "How did you do it?" he exclaimed. The little boy replied, "Oh, Daddy, it was easy. One side of the puzzle is the map of the world, but on the other side is the face of a man. You see, Daddy, if you get the man right, the world will be right." Many people need to realize that if they first get themselves right their world will seem a little better.

Perhaps the apostle Paul gives us the best prescription for the cure of Grouchitis. "Whatsoever things are true, whatsoever things are honest, whatsoever things are just, whatsoever things are pure, whatsoever things are lovely, whatsoever things are of good report; if there be any virtue and if there be any praise, think on these things" (Philippians 4:8 KJV).

Try it—it just might work for you!

26

Answering Pain's "whys"

One of the hardest questions I have to answer as a pastor is the *why?* of the hospital room, the sickbed, the funeral home.

"Why didn't God heal my husband?"

"Why does my innocent child have to suffer so?"

Just this week a desperate young mother came into my office. "Why?" she sobbed. "Why am I dying of cancer and leaving my husband and children behind? Tell me, Pastor, if God loves me so much, *why*?"

It's in those times that I feel most inadequate, void of a profoundly wise answer that will solve all the problems, remove all the questions. But *why*? is not an impossible question if we look in the right place for the answer.

We know that God heals. "I am the God who heals you," He declared to Israel, and He has not changed. Through the psalmist He says, "I forgive all your iniquities and heal all your diseases." Over and over in the New Testament we read that Jesus was moved with compassion and healed the sick.

He opened blind eyes.

He straightened twisted, atrophied limbs.

He cleansed leprous hands and bodies.
He unstopped deaf ears.
He quenched burning fevers in an instant.
He banished screaming demons.
He pulled the plug on pain.
He even brought life back to dead bodies.

Great was the fame and rejoicing over those miracles. It is *wonderful* when tumors are arrested and disappear from X-rays, when cancers cease spreading, when strength and abilities are restored. God be praised, He still does these things today.

But of deeper concern to the loving heart of God is the healing of that part of you that lives forever . . . your soul. The most debilitating and destructive disease that man has is the disease of sin. It results not just in physical pain and weakness, but in eternal, spiritual death.

We were already pronounced dead as a result of our sin (Ephesians 2:1), but there is a cure! His name is Jesus and He heals completely. In the King James Version the words "health" and "salvation" are often interchanged. This is the kind of healing that God is most concerned with. Those who cry out for it are always cured. Unlike poor, uninsured patients in the doorway of the emergency room of a private hospital, they are never turned away.

And they never die. Everyone in the New Testament whom Jesus healed rose from their beds to die another day. No physical healing is permanent—but the spiritual healing He died to provide is eternal.

What do we do, then, when physical sickness comes and God seems silent, when pleas for healing and restoration seem to go unanswered? Ask first, has my soul been healed? Has the main disease been cured? Has the antidote been applied? If so, thank Him for the healing you have already received. Then, know that His heart is moved with compassion at your present pain. He never willingly afflicts His children, but neither does He prevent all suffering.

He knows what He is about. We have the freedom to ask for physical healing.

Ask. *Then leave it in His hands.*

Should God see fit to heal you or your loved one, praise Him for the added days He has graciously given you. But if physical healing does not come—if you are left with weakness and pain where you desired strength, or with an empty place where once the family circle was complete—know that out of what you have experienced will come all the grace and strength you need to meet this trial as His child.

And one day for sure, permanent healing will come.

27

Heart
The Spiritual Beat

One of the wonders beyond comprehension is the human heart.

That little muscle about the size of a fist keeps our bodies alive. The heart weighs less than a pound, yet it has the most challenging job of any organ in the body. The heart beats or contracts from 60 to 80 times a minute, or an average of 72 times a minute, 4320 times an hour, 100,000 times a day, 40 million times a year. Doctors tell us that the heart exerts enough energy every 24 hours to raise a two-pound weight 12 miles into the air. With the beats of the heart are pumped 15 gallons of blood an hour through 100,000 miles of blood vessels within our bodies. It takes a drop of blood about 22 seconds to make its round trip through the circulatory system.

While we go about our daily activities, whatever they may be, our heart keeps on and on. While we sleep it faithfully pumps on, yet we take it for granted or seldom think about the job it's doing. If it should stop its work at any time, we would die. We just cannot live without it.

Our spirit has a heart also. It is spoken of often in the Bible. Where it is and what it is are difficult questions to answer precisely, yet we can be certain that it does exist. The Bible speaks of David's heart. While God spoke to the prophet Samuel about David He said, "Look not on his countenance or on the height of his stature . . . for the Lord seeth not as man seeth; for man looketh on the outward appearance, but the Lord looketh on the heart" (1 Samuel 16:7 KJV).

Solomon was said to have had heart: "God gave Solomon wisdom and exceedingly great understanding, and largeness of heart like the sand on the seashore" (1 Kings 4:29 NKJV). There are different kinds of hearts: bitter hearts, stubborn hearts, jealous hearts, wicked hearts, deceitful hearts. There are hard hearts, soft hearts, sad hearts, and glad hearts. Finally there are kind hearts, loving hearts, clean hearts, righteous hearts, big hearts, gentle hearts, sweet hearts, and, most precious of all, pure hearts.

Blest are the pure in heart,
For they shall see our God;
The secret of the Lord is theirs;
Their soul is His abode.

Still to the lowly soul
He doth himself impart,
And for His service and His throne
Selects the pure in heart.

—John Keble

28

There Is Room . . .

I have never met a person who believed in heaven but didn't want to go there when his time was up. What a glorious city God has promised it to be! No more suffering, no pain, no sorrow; all will be joy forevermore. It is difficult for me as a human to comprehend such a place, much less define it, for as a fellow writer once put it, "Heaven would hardly be heaven if we could define it." Although it is true that it can't be defined, by using the Bible along with simple mathematics we can learn a few facts about that city prepared for the children of God.

When I was a boy, I used to wonder how heaven could possibly be so large that it would hold all the people who were supposed to go there, but these fears soon vanished away when I began to ponder it.

Just look at it. Its length is as large as its width. The city measures 1500 miles in each direction. It has 12 foundations, or floors, each floor named for one of the apostles. About 125 miles separates each floor from the one above it. Mathematicians tell us that if the city were divided into rooms that were one mile wide, one mile high, and one mile long, heaven would be able to contain 3,375,000,000 rooms, each containing the space of one cubic mile. What a city!

But God will not limit our activities to heaven alone, for the Bible states that there will be gates on the east, on the west, on the north, and on the south, so that we can enjoy not only the walls of jasper, gates of pearl, and streets of gold, but the beauty of a perfect universe of galaxies and stars created by the Master Builder.

I have often been asked, "How will we know each other in heaven?" The answer to that question is simple and plain: We will be known as we are known here in this world.

But heaven would not be heaven if it were not for the people in it. And I have met some of the people who are going to be there. I've met them in church services, in camp meetings, in hospitals, in homes for the aged, in youth retreats, in conventions, in Bible conferences, and in their homes. Yes, it's easy to tell those who are real Christians and those who will be among the heavenly citizens.

I have often been asked, "How will we know each other in heaven?" The answer to that question is simple and plain: We will be known as we are known here in this world. Matthew says, "Many will come from east and west and sit down with Abraham, Isaac, and Jacob in the kingdom of heaven" (8:11 NKJV). These men will be recognizable, and so will we.

But as much as there is splendor in that beautiful city built by God, there is also a place of torment, which the Bible calls hell. A place "where the worm dieth not and the fire is not quenched." A place where all suffering and pain—spiritual, mental, and physical—will culminate for eternity. When I think of the differences in these eternal abodes, it is hard to understand how anyone would choose anything less than heaven.

29

His Will

Embracing God's Vision

When I was a teenager I was almost afraid of the will of God. I thought that if I let God rule my life, something terrible would happen: He might send me to darkest Africa or some other remote spot where I would be lonely or fearful. But as I grew in my walk with the Lord, I came to realize that in His will was the perfect plan for my life.

Romans 12:2 reminds us that when we have been transformed by the power of God, we will begin to experience "that good and acceptable and perfect will of God" for our lives (NKJV). When we give up the things of the world in order to live in the will of God, we find that He has replaced the things that once seemed so important to us with things that are far greater and better.

Scripture teaches us that the things of this life will eventually pass away, but he who does the will of God will abide forever. If we really want to make a lasting contribution to this world, we need to release it. For when it loses its grip on us, we will see it in its proper perspective. All that the world has to offer is temporal and passing away.

Only what is done for Christ will stand the test of time. God has forgiven us and brought us into His family so that we might serve Him. He has called us to an act of obedience by which we determine to serve Him at all times.

God never leaves His purposes to guesswork. He clearly tells us in the Bible what He wants us to do. The key to discerning His will is not so much where we go or what we do as *becoming what He wants us to be*. His principles for life are laid out in the Scriptures, which serve as our guide. As we prayerfully seek His guidance, He promises to lead us into each step of life according to His perfect will. We simply must be willing to follow.

It may not be on the mountain's height
Or over the stormy sea;
It may not be at the battle's front
My Lord will have need of me.

But if by a still small voice He calls
To paths I do not know,
I'll answer, dear Lord, with my hand in Thine,
I'll go where You want me to go.

I'll go where You want me to go, dear Lord,
O'er mountain or plain or sea;
I'll say what You want me to say, dear Lord,
I'll be what You want me to be.

—Mary Brown

30

Holy

Our Awe-Inspiring God

What comes to mind when you think of the word *holy*?

Stained-glass windows? Gothic cathedrals? Robes and candles and high-walled convents? Bumbling priests and hypocritical preachers? Hollywood has succeeded in presenting an image of "holiness" that most of the world either scorns or shrugs off as having nothing to do with reality.

Yet to miss understanding the holiness of God is to miss everything.

All that God is He is because He is holy. He loves us because He is holy and can only desire good. He keeps His promises because He is holy and cannot lie. He judges sin because He is holy and cannot abide its presence. Calvary was necessary because of His holiness. His holiness is not merely the absence of sin. It is absolute, blinding perfection.

The holiness of God is a fearful thing. It is far beyond the highest purity we can imagine. Men in the Scriptures who saw God were left prostrate. They were shattered and speechless except for confessing their sinfulness and submission to Him.

Abraham stretched himself upon the ground and was silent.

Moses hid his face in fear.

Isaiah was completely undone and could only confess his uncleanness.

Daniel went into shock. His face turned deathly pale and he grew weak with fright.

John fell at His feet as if dead.

Paul could only gasp, "Lord, what will You have me to do?"

We don't hear much talk about a holy God anymore. Our music and messages today emphasize His love and forgiveness, the acceptance and intimate fellowship we have in Him. God is presented as the secret to our success and the source of all our supply. We have become almost too familiar with Him, too casual in our approach.

I once heard of a young lady who was touring Europe and entered a museum in Vienna. In solitary splendor in a silent, sun-splashed room was the piano of Beethoven. Without thinking the girl sat down and began to peck out a tune. Suddenly one of the museum's guides hurried into the room. He informed the American girl that this was in fact the piano of the great master. He also told her that the great concert pianist Paderewski had recently come to view that very piano.

"And what did Paderewski play?" the girl asked.

"Nothing," said the guide. "He said he was not worthy to touch Beethoven's piano."

I'm afraid we have gotten out of balance in our view of God. We know how to enjoy Him—and well we should—*but we have forgotten how to tremble.*

We know how to rejoice in His blessings—and that is right and proper—*but we have forgotten how to mourn.*

We feel confident in our asking and receiving—and He is pleased with that—*but we have forgotten how to confess.*

We have somehow lost the vision of a holy and almighty God, high and lifted up, terrible and awesome in His greatness. We have lost the resulting sense of our own unworthiness and sinfulness.

And frankly, our lives reveal it.

To His holy people throughout the ages God has said, "Be holy, for I am holy." We are called "saints," literally "holy ones." Peter explains that we have become members of a holy priesthood and holy nation. Paul reminded the Thessalonians that God has not called us to uncleanness but to holiness. He exhorted the Corinthians to perfect holiness in the fear of God.

Very few honest observers would describe the church today as holy. We have tolerated sin and accepted a level of personal righteousness that is little different from that of the world. We do not shrink from sin in horror anymore.

We need a fresh vision of God in His absolute holiness. We need to see Him as the High and Holy One, the inhabiter of all eternity.

Just for a moment, picture yourself attending a beautiful, storybook wedding. The lovely young bride, her face radiant, is just coming down the aisle to stand by her chosen one. Without warning someone across the aisle from you suddenly stands and hurls a water balloon filled with old crankcase oil right at the front of her spotless white gown.

It all happens in an instant. Everyone is stunned. The black oil soaks the young woman's lace bodice, fouls her white gloves, splatters her veil, sends grimy streams down her shocked face, and oozes over her white shoes. Can you see it? The audience gasps in horror—just before the church erupts in outrage and righteous indignation. "What a cruel, horrible, unthinkable thing to do! What an outrage!"

We can feel the emotion over an imaginary scene such as that, but can we begin to imagine heaven's grief over sin within the church, the bride of Jesus Christ? Can we begin to look at sin in our personal lives the way a holy, righteous God views that sin?

To be painfully honest, many of us enjoy sin's attractiveness, flirt with its promises, and accommodate it as much as possible in our daily routines. We do not want to be seen as puritanical or prudish. Sin is hardly mentioned, much less denounced.

Where is the desire for holiness today?

Where is the brokenness over sin that separates from God and grieves His heart?

Where is the fear of offending a holy God that made Isaiah and Daniel and Moses tremble before Him?

We need a fresh vision of God in His absolute holiness. We need to see Him as the High and Holy One, the inhabiter of all eternity. We need to confess Him with the words of Scripture:

> Who among the gods is like you, O LORD? Who is like you—majestic in holiness, awesome in glory, working wonders? (Exodus 15:11).

> There is no one holy like the LORD; there is no one besides you; there is no Rock like our God (1 Samuel 2:2).

Then and only then will we see sin in all its ugliness and offense. Then and only then can true confession take place. Then and only then will we know the mind-staggering grace that makes us partakers of His holiness. Then and only then will the church regain her witness to a lost and dying world.

31

Home

Our Spiritual Destiny

His once-robust body was now spent, his strength gone. Stooped over with the weight of many years, he shuffled along the ship's deck, thinking only of home.

Home—the place were he had grown from infancy to young manhood. The place where he had forged so many friendships, shaped so many memories.

Home—the place he had last seen so many years before. Willingly, eagerly, he had abandoned this beloved land to pursue a new life in a new place. A totally foreign place, dramatically different in nearly every way from his native soil.

While still in his twenties he had sailed to Africa, the fabled dark continent. Compelled by the call of Christ, he gave his life to become a missionary. For more than 40 years he endured rebuke, disease, and myriad dangers to share the gospel with a primitive people. In the early years he met a young lady who also had dedicated her life to serve Christ in Africa. They fell in love, married, and poured themselves wholly into the arduous work.

Now she too was gone. Some years before, malaria had taken her away from him.

He was alone—an older, wizened man returning to the place of his youth. *What will it be like to arrive?* So powerful was the thought that he found himself mouthing the words. *Who will greet me? Will my years of sacrifice be appreciated?*

The thoughts rushed on relentlessly. Soon, over the giant ship's bow he saw the unmistakable New York harbor. It loomed ever closer until, after what seemed an interminable period, the great liner inched into port. Lining the docks were hundreds, perhaps thousands, of cheering well-wishers. One placard read *WELCOME HOME, TEDDY.*

The old man's heart stirred. *Teddy—my own name, he thought. They've come to greet me! They really care! Oh, its great to be home!*

At that instant another remarkable thing happened: A band burst into a rousing rendition of "Hail to the Chief." Then to his right he saw and remembered the real reason for the crowds and fanfare: The President of the United States, Theodore "Teddy" Roosevelt, was disembarking from the ship. He had sailed on this very ship, returning from an African safari.

In no time, it seemed, the crowds were gone. The music faded. The cheers fell silent. For the old missionary there was no one waiting at the dock. No familiar face. No friendly smile. No warm embrace of greeting.

After retrieving his battered baggage, the old man stood still, taking in the sights and sounds and smells of home. But sadness filled his heart, and a feeling of self-pity welled up inside. "Some homecoming," he found himself muttering. Then, as poignant as any message he had heard in his entire life, a voice spoke into the recesses of his troubled heart.

Son, God's voice said lovingly, *just remember . . . you're not yet home.*

How often we are misled into thinking that this life is our destiny and this place is our home.

But of course, it isn't.

We are subjects of another realm.

The apostle Paul reminded the Philippians that "our citizenship is in heaven." At the time he wrote those words, Paul was shackled in a Roman prison; but spiritually he was liberated. He knew that the chains and imprisonment were only temporary inconveniences. One way or another, he would be set free. One way or another, he would go home.

"Our light and momentary troubles," he wrote in his second letter to the Corinthians, "are achieving for us an eternal glory that far outweighs them all. So we fix our eyes not on what is seen, but what is unseen. For what is seen is temporary, but what is unseen is eternal" (2 Corinthians 4:17,18).

Before Jesus returned to His rightful place in heaven, He encouraged His disciples with a promise: "Do not let your hearts be troubled. Trust in God; trust also in me. In my Father's house are many rooms; if it were not so, I would have told you. I am going there to prepare a place for you. And if I go and prepare a place for you, I will come back and take you to be with me" (John 14:1-3).

Don't forget, this promise is for you, too! Whenever you are distracted by this earthly life, remember that every suffering is temporary.

Whenever your physical body is ravaged by disease or begins to wear out with age, remember that you will one day be clothed with an eternal, perfect body.

Whenever you are tempted to accumulate things and place them above people, remember that material things are actually as worthless as wood, hay, and stubble.

Whenever you feel unsettled, worried, or out of place, remember that you *are* out of place.

You're not yet home.

32

Hope

An Antidote for Despair

Shot down in an 1965 combat mission over North Vietnam, naval aviator James B. Stockdale became one of the first P.O.W.'s of that bloody war. During his seven years of captivity Stockdale endured frequent torture. He was chained with his hands over his head for days at a time. His leg was broken by his captors and never properly set, resulting in a permanent limp. He was kept in isolation and allowed to see only his guards and interrogators.

After his release, Stockdale said the only thing that kept him alive was *hope.*

Hope of one day going home.

Hope that each day would be the day of his release.

Without such anticipation, he knew he would have died like so many others.[5]

What an amazing account of human bravery and strength! What an inspiring illustration of the power of hope to sustain life! How difficult it must have been for him to maintain any sense of encouragement as the days followed each other in dreary, painful sameness. After all, he had no real assurance that he would ever be released. There was no precedent, no established pattern, no guarantee he would ever leave that frightful cell.

His was a hope born of desperation. He hoped because there was nothing else he could do.

The world around us is permeated with a sense of hopelessness. Environmentalists tell us the world suffers from "ozone depletion." Other experts debate those claims. But who could debate the ravages of *hope depletion* across our sin-weary planet?

You see it in the gaunt faces of the Ethiopian mothers clutching their starving children.

You see it in the angry eyes of young people trapped in crime-infested ghettos.

You see it in the wasted forms dying in cancer wards.

They have no reason to believe relief will come, that things will be different. Should anyone dare to hope, it becomes little more than a positive mental attitude, a shallow effort at "happy talk" against a curtain of overwhelming despair. People may talk of hope for peace in the Middle East or for a cure for AIDS. But it's like throwing matches against the darkness. Hope might glimmer for a moment, but its light is soon quenched. The Bible plainly states that those who are without Christ, who are foreigners when it comes to His promises, are without hope. They have no reason for confidence or assurance about anything.

While the world uses "hope" to express a wish, a desire, or a dream, the Bible uses the word to mean a *confident expectation* of something future and unseen. It is something we simply wait on, knowing it will come. There is not the least question about it. It is certain. It can be counted on.

The Bible talks about—

> the hope of the *resurrection*
> the hope of the *promise*

the hope of *righteousness*
the hope of the *glory of God*
the hope of *salvation*
the hope of *His calling*
the hope of *eternal life*
the *blessed hope and glorious appearing* of
our Lord Jesus Christ.

Substitute the word "assurance" or "conviction" for each of these things and you will grasp the biblical essence of hope.

You see, unlike Mr. Stockdale in his prison cell, we have a solid reason for our hope. Our certainty wraps itself in a Person—the Lord Jesus Christ. He is our hope and glory, our precedent, our pattern, our guarantee. Peter tells us that His resurrection brought us into the living hope in which we stand. It secured for us an incorruptible, undefiled inheritance that even now awaits us in heaven. Hebrews tells us our hope is sure because Jesus has entered into the sanctuary made without hands, fulfilling the promise God made and swore to by Himself. This hope is an anchor for our souls, steadfast and sure because of what He has done.

The Word of God confirms our hope. Paul told the Romans, "Everything that was written in the past was written to teach us, so that through endurance and the encouragement of the Scriptures we might have hope" (Romans 15:4). The psalmist continually spoke of his hope in God's Word as the antidote, the corrective for the despair that would threaten his soul. All that is written in the Word is there to confirm our trust in God: fulfilled prophecies, kept promises, testimonies of those whose trust in God was rewarded. All of these are preserved in written form so that we might *know* beyond the shadow of a doubt that God keeps His Word.

Is it any wonder the psalmist cried within his heart, "Why are you downcast, O my soul? Why so disturbed within me?" (Psalm 42:11).

Do you find yourself discouraged? Ready to quit? Do depression and despair have you in their grip? Go to the Living Word, Jesus, and the written Word, the Scriptures. The hope you will find there is all you will ever need. Never forget and always believe, whatever your need may be . . . there's hope for your troubled times.

33

Jesus

The Name Fulfilled

Jesus is the Greek name in the New Testament which translates the Old Testament Hebrew name *Joshua,* which means "savior" or "deliverer." It is the perfect name for Christ, since He, like the Old Testament leader Joshua, was the leader of His people. The term *Christ* is taken from the Greek *christos,* meaning "anointed one" or "messiah." Thus Jesus is our Lord's personal name and Christ is His title.

The importance of Jesus' name is emphasized in Scripture, which says, "Therefore God also has highly exalted Him and given Him the name which is above every name, that at the name of Jesus every knee should bow . . . and that every tongue should confess that Jesus Christ is Lord, to the glory of God the Father" (Philippians 2:10, 11 NKJV).

I have news for you: Everyone will one day acknowledge the lordship and authority of Christ! The Communist leaders will be forced to acknowledge Him. The cultic followers of Sun Myung Moon, the "moonies," will bow down before Him. The Buddhists, the Muslims, the Hindus, and all the rest will kneel before Jesus Christ and proclaim Him King of kings and Lord of lords.

There are many things about the name of Jesus that make it very special. Here are three of the most important ones.

1. *Jesus is a name from heaven.*

The angel who appeared to Mary told her what to name the baby: "Behold, you will conceive in your womb and bring forth a Son, and shall call His name Jesus" (Luke 1:31 NKJV). God chose His name and sent His angel to announce that name.

The name for "savior" was the perfect name for God's incarnate Son. The Bible says of that name, "Neither is there salvation in any other, for there is no other name under heaven given among men whereby we must be saved" (Acts 4:12 KJV). No other name, not Edward, Richard, or Robert, can bring salvation. Only the name of Jesus can save.

2. *Jesus is a name of hope.*

No other name can bring such hope of forgiveness and deliverance from sin. There is power in the name of Jesus. His is a name of hope that brings confidence and reassurance to the hearts of all people.

One of my responsibilities as a pastor is to visit people in the hospital. Whenever I visit with someone there, I discover that everyone seems to think he or she has the best doctor in Atlanta. "Pastor, I hear that he is the best doctor in town," they often say. I've never yet met someone who told me his was the "worst doctor in town." The patients brag about the doctor, the hospital, and the nurses.

But when I mention the name of Jesus, all other names pale into insignificance. He alone brings a sparkle to the eyes and joy to the heart. The very mention of His name causes a smile to come to people's lips and a ray of hope into their hearts. Whenever I get down or discouraged, I whisper the name of Jesus, and hope swells up in my own heart as well.

3. *Jesus is a name of honor.*

Jesus' name is associated with victory and deliverance. Just as Joshua, His Old Testament namesake, conquered the Promised Land and drove out Israel's enemies, so Jesus has conquered Satan's power and given us eternal life in heaven. As Joshua marched through the land of Canaan, his very name brought the hope of deliverance to the Israelites and struck fear in the hearts of their enemies.

The demons trembled before Jesus Christ. "What have we to do with thee?" they cried. Satan could not tempt Him to sin. Rome could not conquer Him. The scribes could not outwit Him. Even the crucifixion could not stop Him. Jesus came to this earth to die for our sins and rise again the third day. In so doing He trampled underfoot the very head of Satan himself, opening the way for all who choose to live the joyful Christian life.

A young man in our church recently said, "Pastor, I don't know what to do; it's just getting better all the time." As he talked about his faith in Christ and his relationship with Him, tears of joy trickled down his face.

"You don't have to worry about what to do." I replied. "Just go ahead and enjoy it!"

We don't have to wait to get to heaven to enjoy our salvation; we have already been made citizens of the heavenly kingdom. We have eternal life within our hearts. The Promised Land is already in our possession, and we need to live our spiritual lives to the fullest extent.

Jesus too had a Promised Land:
It wasn't a place,
It was a plan.

34

Joy

Rejoicing in Chains

Prisons today are five-star resorts compared to those in which Paul languished.

He enjoyed no heated cell with private toilet and sink. There was no mattress for sleeping, no TV room for relaxing, no well-stocked library for reading and study. There was only the dark encasement of roughly hewn stones, filled with putrid odors and the pungent reminders of human depravity. Perhaps worst of all were the chains, their rusty coarseness scraping his skin raw, constantly tugging at him. And the sounds—every day he heard them—cries of tortured souls who wished only to die.

As if imprisonment were not painful enough, Paul had to endure something worse: the stinging criticism of those who called themselves his Christian brothers. They dared to attack God's apostle even while he was held captive for the sake of Christ.

Stop, please, and imagine yourself in Paul's situation. Feel the weight of the chains on raw skin. Taste the nauseating swill that was his daily food. Listen to those dreadful sounds of suffering that filled his ears day and night. Look into the menacing eyes of the Roman prison guards who threatened with their very presence.

You are there. You are suffering. You are chained. You are Paul the apostle. Now . . . what's your attitude? What fills your heart through the weary hours, stretching into months and years?

Here's what Paul wrote to his friends in Philippi:

> I want you to know, brothers, that what has happened to me has really served to advance the gospel. As a result, it has become clear throughout the whole palace guard and to everyone else that I am in chains for Christ. Because of my chains, most of the brothers in the Lord have been encouraged to speak the word of God more courageously and fearlessly (Philippians 1:12-14).

What an attitude! Rather than being inflamed with furious self-pity, Paul is encouraged by the positive impact of his negative condition.

Throughout his message to the Philippians a thread is evident, a golden thread through the letter's fabric. It reverberates through the letter like the repeating theme of a Beethoven symphony . . . now subtly in the background, now breaking out in a triumphant, symphonic burst.

The theme is joy.

Abundant, victorious joy. Joy that supersedes suffering and overcomes obstacles. Joy that endures. More than 70 times in this brief epistle, Paul uses the word "joy" or its cognates to express his truest feelings and deepest desires.

Paul does not say that he is happy, for that wasn't true. He wasn't happy to be in prison. He wasn't happy to be separated from friends and loved ones. He wasn't happy to be wrongly criticized. But he was joyful. Happiness is a feeling completely dependent on one's situation or condition. Joy, however, is something quite different, for it is never held prisoner by one's lot in life.

Happiness deals with the externals, joy with what is within. Joy is the ever-abiding confidence that all is well regardless of the outward circumstance, because our loving God is in control. You can be sick, yet joyful. Handicapped, yet joyful. Attacked, yet joyful.

The apostle Paul was joyful. Why? Because the deepest desire of his heart was being fulfilled even while he languished in his cell: The Good News of Jesus Christ was catching fire all over the Roman world.

Persecution wasn't stopping it.

Threats and executions weren't stopping it.

Even his own chains weren't stopping it.

Right there in his corner of the prison, news had spread throughout the whole palace guard that he was chained because of the name of Jesus.

Paul was also joyful because Christians were being encouraged to speak God's Word.

> It means that most of our brothers, taking fresh heart in the Lord from the very fact that I am a prisoner for Christ's sake, have shown far more courage in boldly proclaiming the Word of God (Philippians 1:14 PHILLIPS).

Many who saw Paul's boldness drew strength from his compelling life and witness. Bravery has a magnetic effect which motivates others to get involved. Of course, not all are so affected. There were Christians in Paul's day, as in our own, who were propelled by perverted motives and selfish intentions, attempting to diminish the apostle's influence through a smear campaign.

How did he respond? "What does it matter?" he asks. "The important thing is that in every way, whether from false motives or true, Christ is preached. And because of this I rejoice" (Philippians 1:18).

Paul's concerns boiled down to one thing: He was not striving for personal power or success. He wanted only to see the power of the gospel unleashed across the world like water roaring out of a broken dam. When he saw it, his heart was filled with joy.

So it should be for us. Whatever our circumstances, whatever our condition, Jesus Christ should be the source of our satisfaction. For He is our joy. And when He occupies the right place in our hearts, everything else will fit properly, and we will experience true, deep, abiding joy.

35

Kindness

The Willing Sacrifice

David and Jonathan.

Their names are virtual synonyms for friendship. So strong was the bond between these men that each was willing to make any sacrifice for the other.

Jonathan was the oldest son of Saul, King of Israel. Although the apparent heir to the throne, Jonathan knew that God had chosen his closest friend, David, to be the next king. Out of his deep love for the young shepherd, Jonathan made a covenant with him and gave him his own robe, tunic, sword, bow, and belt—the very symbols of his regal standing. When King Saul attempted to capture David to kill him, Jonathan thwarted his father's plans and helped David escape.

When they last saw each other, Jonathan said to David, "Show me unfailing kindness like that of the LORD as long as I live, so that I may not be killed, and do not ever cut off your kindness from my family—not even when the LORD has cut off every one of David's enemies from the face of the earth."

In battle with the Philistines at Mount Gilboa, Jonathan was killed, as were his father and two brothers. When news of their deaths reached David, he was torn by grief. In his mourning he wrote, "I grieve for you, Jonathan my brother; you were very dear to me. Your love for me was wonderful, more wonderful than that of women."

David assumed the kingship of Israel, but he never forgot Jonathan nor the kindness he had promised his beloved friend.

Some time later, after the son of Jesse had conquered his foes and established his kingdom, his thoughts drifted back to his loyal and valiant friend. He asked, "Is there anyone still left of the house of Saul to whom I can show kindness for Jonathan's sake?" (2 Samuel 9:1).

The answer came from a servant, who informed David that Jonathan's sole heir was a crippled son named Mephibosheth. Without delay King David called for the young man to be brought to him.

With great fear Mephibosheth entered the king's presence, bowing low before him.

"Don't be afraid," David said to him, "for I will surely show you kindness for the sake of your father Jonathan. I will restore to you all the land that belonged to your grandfather Saul, and you will always eat at my table."

Kindness is a fruit of the Spirit-controlled life, and not something to which we are naturally inclined. Daily, consciously, we must seek out opportunities to show kindness, for in doing so we express the very character of Christ.

Humbled before the powerful king, Mephibosheth asked, "What is your servant, that you should notice a dead dog like me?"

Using the most contemptible description—dead dog—he referred to himself as an utterly useless person. Not only physically handicapped, Mephibosheth also bore the social stigma of belonging to Saul's discredited family. But that mattered not at all to David. He saw more than the lame body of a social outcast. In Mephibosheth he saw a person to whom he could repay Jonathan's love and kindness.

Who are the Mephibosheths in your life?

Who are those to whom you could be a source of encouragement? Chances are that there are many who fit this category. Some may be handicapped physically, as was Mephibosheth. But it is more likely they are handicapped emotionally or spiritually, suffering because they feel unloved and unwanted. However, they all have something in common: They need you. They need your concern, your touch, your tender words.

They need your kindness.

And what about those you know best, the members of your own family? Are you showing even the simplest of kindnesses to them?

How easily we take for granted those nearest to us, those who have likely done the most for us! This is, unfortunately, a trait of sinful human nature. We are wise to remember that kindness is a fruit of the Spirit-controlled life, and not something to which we are naturally inclined. Daily, consciously, we must seek out opportunities to show kindness, for in doing so we express the very character of Christ.

Finally, what about your own response to God's kindness?

Luke describes the occasion when Jesus passed through a village on His way to Jerusalem and stopped when ten lepers cried out for His help. He commanded them to go to the priest for examination. On their way the diseased-ravaged men were miraculously healed, freed from leprosy's pitiless bondage. One of them, a Samaritan, realized he was healed and went back to Jesus, praising God in a loud voice.

Throwing himself at Jesus' feet, he thanked Him greatly. Jesus asked, "Were not all ten cleansed? Where are the other nine?" Although He had shown amazing kindness for them, only one returned to show gratitude.

Each day's dawning is a fresh opportunity for every one of us to whisper, "Thank You, Lord, for Your wonderful kindness to me!" If you do this, you'll be prepared to think God's way . . . and show His kindness to those who cross your pathway.

36

Known

An Intimate Savior and Friend

There is one fact that all Christians can take confidence in, and it is this: We are known by God. Our heavenly Father has not forsaken us in this world, leaving us to face all the heartaches, troubles, and trials alone, but He is always near and ready to help us through life's hard places. The Bible tells us that even the hairs of our head are numbered and that God keeps a record of all we ever say or do. He knows more about us than anyone else with whom we are involved. All of us have family and friends in whom we place our trust, those with whom we share our most guarded secrets and otherwise confidential matters, but what they know about us is very little when compared to the knowledge that God has of us.

Not only does He know all about us, but He cares all about us as well. No matter what we have done, no matter how low we have fallen and miserably failed, He will always be there to forgive and come to our rescue. What a blessed hope this is, that the Christian faith is a personal faith with a personal Savior and personal Friend!

A loving friend is Jesus,
Kindhearted, faithful, and true,
A friend who is always near us
To help and bring us through.

A loving friend is Jesus,
Our comforter and guide,
One who never leaves us,
Who is walking by our side.

A loving friend is Jesus;
Though often we are weak,
He understands and pardons
When we forgiveness seek.

—Author unknown

I once heard the story of a census-taker who happened upon a small house far back in the country. Knocking on the door, he was greeted by a small, silver-haired woman. "Yes, sir," she said; "what can I do for you?" After a short introduction about the purpose of his visit he asked, "What is the number of your children, ma'am?" Somewhat confused about what the man had said, she replied, "Mista, my chilun ain't got no numbers, they only got names!" Likewise it is with God's children: He knows them by their names.

37

Listening

Loving Without Words

In the early days of this century a steamship company advertised for a telegraph operator. On the day interviews were to be given, anxious job-seekers crowded the company waiting room. Every seat was taken, compelling latecomers to stand wherever space was available. Quiet talk and chatter filled the time, but as the hour for interviewing came and passed, no one from the company appeared. A wave of restlessness rippled through the room.

Suddenly one man leaped from his chair, opened the door to the inner office, and disappeared inside. A loud murmuring began that only grew more intense as the minutes ticked by.

Finally a company official opened the door. "Thank you all for coming today," he said. "The position has been filled."

Quieting the angry comments, he went on to explain. "From the time interviews were set to begin, we have been broadcasting in Morse code over our intercom the instructions to come into the inner office and ask for Mr. James. This gentleman here was the only one who heard those instructions. He has earned the job."

How much we lose because we do not listen! These men lost their opportunity because they were broadcasting to each other when they should have been receiving. Marriages have broken down because one partner talks too much, the other not enough. Parents and teens remain isolated in their separate worlds, unable to touch, because each feels the other doesn't really listen. Miscommunication has bungled many a business deal and strained many a friendship. We all speak our minds so freely these days, but are we as generous with our listening as we are with our talking?

James wrote some very wise words on this subject: "My dear brothers, take note of this: Everyone should be quick to listen, slow to speak and slow to become angry" (James 1:19).

Did you catch that progression? If we are quick to listen, more interested in hearing what the other person says than planning our answer, it only follows that we will be slow to speak. If we are slow to speak, thinking about our words, using them with care, it only follows that we will have better success in speaking without anger and harshness.

Understanding comes only as we listen, not as we speak. True ministry begins with hearing, not with talking. We don't have to say much at all when someone knows he or she has been heard and understood. Job complained that his three friends tormented and crushed him with words (Job 19:2). How often we do this to each other! How we need to remember that people don't care how much we know until they know how much we care.

Listening is one of the most loving things we can do for one another. Listening with the heart can stop a quarrel before it begins. It can melt hearts hardened by years of pain and bitterness. It can lift many a weight and calm many a fear. It can open avenues of communication barricaded by selfishness and misunderstanding.

And let's not forget another kind of listening we need to practice: listening to God. His still, small voice is often crowded out by our busyness, even our service for Him. Our inattention to His speaking can make us miss many opportunities, just like the men in the steamship office. He is always there, always speaking.

The world is a frantic, noisy place. Learn to slip away from the clamor and be silent. Don't feel the compulsion to fill every quiet space with words. Rediscover the art of listening to your Lord. And in your relationships, stop your hurrying and your talking. Instead, look at those around you who need someone to care. Listen with your ears and your heart to what they are saying.

Love them . . . without a word.

You'll be amazed at what will happen!

38

Love

Restoration's Expression

In one of the top pop songs of the last decade, "What's Love Got to Do with It?" raspy-voiced singer Tina Turner belted out the words, "What's love but a secondhand emotion?"

Only a few days after the record hit the market, it was number one from coast to coast.

And it made me wonder: Does that actually represent our nation's attitude toward love? A "secondhand emotion"? Are we really that far from what God says about love?

I know of no better place to grip the strong rope of truth about love than in Jesus Himself.

What's love got to do with Him? Just everything.

In the final days of His earthly ministry, just before He died as the substitute for sinners, Jesus told His followers of the one compelling characteristic of the true disciple:

> A new commandment I give you: Love one another. As I have loved you, so you must love one another. By this all men will know that you are my disciples, if you love one another (John 13:34,35).

So simple, isn't it? We show ourselves as true followers of Christ not by the fish symbols on our bumpers or the crosses on our necklaces, but by the demonstration of genuine love. According to Jesus, this is the constant distinguishing mark, unaffected by any other factors.

The significance of what Jesus told His disciples about love is underscored by another incident, reported to us in chapter 22 of Matthew's Gospel. As had become a common occurrence, Jesus was being confronted by the Pharisees, the most prominent Hebrew sect.

Smug, self-righteous men, the Pharisees lived by the letter rather than the spirit of the law. Of course, they rejected Jesus as the Messiah. To them He was nothing but a scheming liar and deceiver who had to be stopped at all costs.

They tried repeatedly to entrap Him, as was the case in this instance. A lawyer of the Pharisees tried to snare Jesus into answering the much-debated question "Which is the greatest commandment in the Law?" Jesus' reply not only confounded the Pharisees but also defined in unmistakable terms the very essence of the entire Old Testament.

Jesus answered: "'Love the Lord your God with all your heart and with all your soul and with all your mind.' This is the first and greatest commandment. And the second is like it: 'Love your neighbor as yourself.' All the Law and the Prophets hang on these two commandments" (Matthew 22:37-40).

With eloquent, powerful simplicity Jesus reduced all of the law and all of the writings of the prophets to two basic commands:

Love God. Love others.

So important is our need to demonstrate true Christian love that an entire chapter of Paul's first letter to the

Corinthians is devoted to the subject. Writing to brothers in Christ who were deeply divided and unloving, Paul said that without love even the most esteemed qualities are meaningless.

Eloquence without love is nothing but a big noise.

Knowledge without love is nothing but an empty intellectual exercise.

Faith without love is worse than useless.

Even sacrifice without love accomplishes precisely zero.

What characterizes true Christian love? Paul described it in 1 Corinthians 13:4-8: Love is patient. Love is kind. Love does not envy, nor does it boast. Love is not proud. Love is not rude or self-seeking. Love is not easily angered, nor does it keep a record of wrongs. Love does not delight in evil but rejoices with the truth. Love always protects, always trusts, always hopes, always perseveres. Love never fails.

When we practice this kind of love we exemplify the very character of Christ and nature of God. In our natural, sinful selves we have no capacity to express such love; it is only through the regenerating power of God that we are able to do so. Our natural tendency is not to be loving, but the Spirit of God within us produces this fruit above all others. In Paul's letter to the church at Galatia he declared that "the fruit of the Spirit is love." It exists and is expressed in our behavior only through His power.

Most wonderful of all is the truth that God loves us *fully and unconditionally*. While we were yet sinners, He loved us and gave Himself as a sacrifice for us. While we yet sin and disobey Him, He loves us and restores us as a tender shepherd. And though we are unable to comprehend such love, through Him we are able to practice it.

George Matheson was a bright, promising young musician when he received the most devastating news of his life: He was going blind.

For several months, as his vision worsened, he had suspected the worst. But more painful than the crushing reality of his blindness was the reaction of his fiancee. When he told her of his condition, she tearfully returned the engagement ring. She said she could not live the rest of her life with a blind man.

Stunned by her rejection and overwhelmed with self-pity, Matheson was reeling like a boxer falling to the mat. But then it was as if he were literally swept into God's arms, encouraged and uplifted. Still disappointed, yet buoyed in spirit, Matheson sat down and composed a song.

In one poignant moment George Matheson knew more deeply than ever what is the true mark of the Christian—the unmistakable mark of love.[6]

That's what his song was all about. It's a song sung by believers all over the world to this day: *O Love That Wilt Not Let Me Go.* Through a hurtful trial, George Matheson was reminded of the love that would remain forever unaffected. In so doing he was able even to love the one who had rejected him, as his Lord had loved those who took His very life.

39

Mercy: The Gift of Forgiveness

A distraught mother appeared before the great Emperor Napoleon, seeking a pardon for her condemned son.

"It is his second offense against me," the Emperor sniffed. "And therefore justice demands his death."

"I don't ask for justice," the mother wept. "I plead for mercy."

"He doesn't deserve mercy!"

"Sir," she continued bravely through her tears, "it would not be mercy if he deserved it, and mercy is all I ask."

"Well, then, since you put it that way," said the emperor, "I will show mercy." And her son was saved.[7]

Napoleon saw immediately the mother's reasoning: You receive mercy only when you do not receive what you deserve. The dictionary tells us that mercy is a refraining, a withholding of harm or punishment due offenders. It is a disposition to be kind, to show pity and to forgive. Napoleon may have granted mercy for the glory it would bring him rather than out of any real concern for the mother or her son, but he still saw the essence of it.

The Scriptures tell us that God is the Father of mercies.

If you said Henry Ford was the father of the Model T, what would it mean? If you said Steven Jobs was the father of the personal computer, what would that mean? It would mean that these men took the seed of an idea from their minds and over the months and years fashioned something with their hands that was a unique representation of those creative thoughts.

What then does the Bible mean when it calls our God "the Father of mercies"? It means that mercy was His idea. He is the One who fashioned it. Better than anyone else, He knows what it really looks like and what it really means. All other mercies in the world are only copies and echoes of His mercy.

The Old Testament brims with descriptions of His mercies. In the King James Version they are said to be manifold (Nehemiah 9:19,27), tender (Psalm 103:4), and sure (Isaiah 55:3). There is a multitude of them (Psalm 69:16). They reach to the heavens (Psalm 57:10) and fill the earth (Psalm 136). The New Testament describes Him as a God who is "rich in mercy" (Ephesians 2:4). Christ is our merciful and faithful High Priest (Hebrews 2:17).

We are encouraged in Hebrews to come boldly to His throne of grace to obtain His mercy (Hebrews 4:16).

There can be no doubt that mercy surrounds our God like a cloud. It is as much a part of His being as His holiness or His power.

It was at a dinner in the home of the despised tax-collector, Matthew, that the Lord Jesus spoke of mercy. The Pharisees were horrified that He would spend time with sinners, eating with them and sharing Himself with them. He overheard their complaints to His disciples. Turning to them, He said, "It is not the healthy who need a doctor, but the sick. But go and learn what this means: 'I desire mercy, not sacrifice.' For I have not come to call the righteous, but sinners" (Matthew 9:13).

What a glorious truth! It is all right to need the mercy of God! That is why Christ came to earth. God's desire is to withhold the just punishment we deserve and give us instead salvation, pardon, and forgiveness. We need not ever fear crying out for His mercy. We don't need to justify ourselves before Him. He knows that we are ill, in need of a physician. He came for us, sickened and weakened and condemned by sin. Mercy is what He is waiting to bestow!

Understanding the mercy of God will make a tremendous difference in how you come to Him.

Come with your needs.

Come with your failures and mistakes.

Come with your sins.

He waits for you to come.

And it will help you in living with others. You have been shown incredible mercy; why not pass it along? Others will treat you badly. They will richly deserve your condemnation, your anger, your tit for tat, your withdrawal of friendship and affection.

But mercy will delight in giving them what they do not deserve:

Forgiveness.

40

New

Reborn by the Spirit

NEW. All of us enjoy things that are clean, fresh, and new. And so does God. That is why He has promised a new birth and a new beginning for all who will believe in Christ. The prophet Ezekiel explains it like this: "A new heart also will I give you, and a new spirit will I put within you" (Ezekiel 36:26 KJV). This incredible promise is one of a new nature.

Throughout the life of a person without Christ, he or she has been controlled by the old nature of sin, but now God promises to give him a new nature. Day in and day out, the only nature he has ever known was that old fleshly nature of sin and self, but now God tells us that a new nature can be ours.

I remember how as a boy my heart was convicted by the Holy Spirit that I was a sinner. I came to realize that I was personally responsible for my sin. I also realized that I could not change my sinful nature and that I could in no way save myself. But just as I was convicted of my sin, I was also convinced that Jesus Christ died for my sins and made my salvation possible. I repented of my sin and by faith turned to Christ to save me. I believe that His death was the sufficient payment for my sins. What I experienced was a new birth in Him. It was a spiritual rebirth that theologians call *regeneration*.

It was the issue of the new birth that was the central topic of Jesus' discussion with Nicodemus, a Jewish religious leader, the main character of discussion in John chapter 3. Our Lord told Nicodemus that he needed the regenerating work of the Holy Spirit within his heart. He put it this way: "Except a man be born again, he cannot see the kingdom of God" (John 3:3 KJV). When Nicodemus questioned how a person could reenter his mother's womb, Christ explained that He was speaking of a spiritual birth (John 3:5).

In discussing this issue, Jesus made it clear that what is "born of the flesh is flesh" and that what is "born of the Spirit is spirit" (John 3:6). The nature of the flesh cannot of itself produce the nature of the Spirit. Only the Spirit of God can do that within our hearts. This is the great news of the Bible: God does for us what we cannot do for ourselves. He gives us His Spirit and regenerates our old fleshly hearts with a brand-new life.

What a reason to celebrate! What a motive for rejoicing! Just think of it:

Old things have passed away and all things have become NEW! (see 2 Corinthians 5:17 KJV).

41

Overcomers

God's Promise of Escape

"*The tempter came to him and said* . . ." (Matthew 4:3).

Even in the life of Jesus we see that temptation came. It always comes, and when it comes it demands a decision. All that a person possesses, all that he claims to be, all the confidence that others have in him, all the confidence he has within himself—everything that is worthwhile in a person's life—depends on what he does when the tempter comes. He has the choice of yielding to the temptation and perhaps ruining all he has ever hoped for, or else overcoming the temptation and thereby proving himself a better person.

Nothing reveals the truth about how to overcome temptation than the scene that took place between Jesus and the devil.

After being baptized by John the Baptist, Jesus went into the wilderness to be tempted of the devil. During this time He was tempted to turn stones into bread to satisfy His hunger, to cast Himself from the top of a high pinnacle of the temple and let his angels bear him safely to the ground as a show of His power, and finally to gain all the world by yielding to the tempter.

As if this were not enough, the Bible states that Jesus was tempted in all points that a man could be tempted in (Hebrews 4:15). In other words, every temptation that comes into our lives Christ faced and overcame. Remember, it is not a sin to be *tempted;* the sin comes when we *yield to the temptation* rather than overcoming it.

Never look for temptation, since temptation will look for you.

One way we can overcome temptation is by simply avoiding exposure to it. There is an old story of a cowboy who decided to stop drinking in order to keep his wife and save his marriage. He tried very hard and was successful for awhile, but each time he went into town he would hitch his horse to the hitching post in front of the saloon. Needless to say, after awhile the temptation was too great and he went back to his old habit. This is the parable of many lives: They need to change their hitching posts! Never look for temptation, since temptation will look for you. We must ever be on guard not to expose ourselves to the people, places, or things that would tempt us to do wrong.

Trochilus, a friend of Plato, was saved from a terrible storm at sea. His boat sank and his crew died, but he was rescued by a miracle from the raging waters. Upon returning home the first thing he did was wall up the windows in his bedchamber that faced the sea. His fear was that some beautiful morning he would arise to view the beauty of the water and again be lured out to sea.

There are windows in many of our lives which face some sea of temptation. It would be good for us to wall them up. We pray in the Lord's Prayer, "Lead us not into temptation" but let us not lead *ourselves* into temptation!

It is good for us to know that no matter what temptation comes our way, through the help of God we can overcome it. We read in 1 Corinthians 10:13, "No temptation has taken you except such as is common to man; but God is faithful, who will not allow you to be tempted beyond what you are able, but with the temptation will also make the way of escape, that you may be able to bear it" (NKJV). It is not necessary for any of us to yield—we have God's Word on it! Think about it: *We always have a way of escape.* The promise of God is true: If we choose to be, we are overcomers!

How beautifully the story of the temptation of Jesus ends: "Then the devil left Him, and behold, angels came and ministered to Him" (Matthew 4:11 NKJV).

42

Patience

Reacting Like Jesus

Do you ever have trials and problems? Of course you do! There's no such thing as a trouble-free life, even for the rich and the very bright. We all endure difficulties, and sometimes Christians must endure more than unbelievers. That was certainly the case in the first century, when one could be fed to the lions for simply claiming allegiance to Jesus Christ. To believers living then, James wrote: "Consider it pure joy, my brothers, whenever you face trials of many kinds, because you know that the testing of your faith develops perseverance [patience]" (1:2).

The vital question is not *whether* we will have trials, but how one will respond to the trials that come. It is often true that character is revealed more in reactions than in actions. God's will is that we react to life's testings like Jesus did—with patience and perseverance. James 1:4 says to "let patience have its perfect work, that you may be perfect and complete, lacking nothing" (NKJV).

The perfection this refers to is not some state of sinlessness but the attainment of spiritual maturity. God wants His children to grow up in faith, becoming complete in Christ, fully equipped for service. This measure of maturity results in part from the believer's response to the trials of faith. These trials may come in countless ways, but always for the same purpose: our perfecting as God's children.

Until his death in 1958, my mother's brother, George Hitt, was a silhouette artist of world renown. He would use a special black paper, and through the process of his own imagination he would create a beautiful scene. With no preliminary drawings, but simply envisioning the finished product in his mind, he would use surgical scissors to cut the silhouette—with all its intricacies—out of the black paper.

The results were astonishing. His silhouettes seemed almost three-dimensional. Pictures seemed to climb out of the page.

It might be the silhouette of a dancer gracefully moving across the stage, a deer standing in a flowery meadow, or even the portrait of some famous individual. In fact, it was his skill in portraits that caused President Franklin D. Roosevelt to invite George to the White House to do silhouette profiles of the entire Roosevelt family. His cuttings hang in the White House today.

During his day, George was proclaimed by many to be one of the greatest silhouette artists in the world. *Guidepost* ran stories on his accomplishments and Robert Ripley made him a topic of *Ripley's Believe It or Not.*

But what was so special about my uncle was not that he was an artist of unparalleled skill, nor that he had received worldwide acclaim.

My uncle was severely disabled—so crippled he could barely move.

As a young man his body was devastated by rheumatoid arthritis. The incurable disease clamped his head, arms, legs, and feet in a viselike grip. Confined to his bed or wheelchair, he could not feed or dress himself. *The only movement he had in his body was the slight use of his left arm and thumb.* Yet with special surgical scissors placed tightly between his thumb and index finger, he captured scenes and characters in silhouette with unbelievable precision and reality.

If anyone knew about trials and difficulty, George did.

As I think of my uncle, I think of how easy it would have been for him to become bitter, or to sink in some state of self-pity, questioning the circumstances of life and the hand of God. Yet as a boy in the presence of my uncle, never once did I hear such a thing fall from his lips. He often talked about the better days ahead, when there would be no more pain and suffering, but would quickly add that for the moment he was going to use his crippled body for the Lord's service.

Though under a perpetual shadow of dark suffering, George Hitt went on painfully shaping black shadows into silhouettes of matchless beauty . . . for the glory of his God.

James says, "Blessed is the man who perseveres under trial, because when he has stood the test, he will receive the crown of life that God has promised to those who love him."

What a marvelous assurance! God will reward us eternally for the pain we endure for His sake in this temporal life.

Many have gone before us, and they wait, gathered as a "great cloud of witnesses," to see how we will finish. The best strategy, says the writer of Hebrews, is to "throw off everything that hinders and the sin that so easily entangles, and let us run with perseverance the race marked out for us." He then gives us the most compelling challenge: "Let us fix our eyes on Jesus, the author and perfecter of our faith, who for the joy set before him endured the cross, scorning its shame, and sat down at the right hand of the throne of God. Consider him who endured such opposition from sinful men, so that you will not grow weary and lose heart" (Hebrews 12:1-3).

Only by patiently following the example of Christ can we experience true victory. Only by looking to Him can we keep perspective. When trials and troubles come, as surely they will, we need to remember that they serve a purpose far beyond what we might imagine. They are being used by the Master Artist as He crafts us into masterpieces for His glory.

43

Peace

A Direct Result of Submission

Over 25 years ago, United Nations Secretary General U Thant called a special meeting. Included in the gathering were 67 scholars and statesmen from 19 countries.

Looking gravely over the podium at that blue-chip panel of the world's best thinkers and diplomats, the Secretary General posed three pointed questions. They were not questions that could be answered before the lunch break.

Nor have they been answered to this day.

"What element is lacking," U Thant asked those men and women, "so that with all our skill and all our knowledge we still find ourselves in the dark valley of discord and enmity?"

No one raised a hand. No one ventured an answer.

He went on. "What is it that inhibits us from going forward together to enjoy the fruits of human endeavor and to reap the harvest of human potential?"

Still no reply. Sixty-seven scholars wearing 67 language headsets frowned and studied their fingernails.

U Thant paused, then asked a final question.

"Why is world peace still a distant objective seen only dimly through the storms and turmoil of our present difficulties?"

Brilliant as he was, the Secretary did not have the answers to the questions he posed. Neither did 67 wise men and women from every corner of the globe.[8]

Like most people, they did not comprehend the fundamental nature of peace nor see its source. The great U.N. leader was looking for peace on a national and international scale, failing to recognize that it is essentially a matter of the individual heart. He viewed peace as a social attainment, not a spiritual fruit.

Our world's preoccupation with peace is evident in the pages of any major newspaper. There we can read of the Middle East peace talks, of the Central American peace accords, and of the pursuit for peace among warring factions in Northern Ireland, in India and Pakistan, and in a hundred more places.

Bumper stickers plead for us to "Visualize World Peace" or to support Greenpeace or other "peace" organizations. Once each year the Nobel Peace Prize is announced with much fanfare and exhaustive reports in the media. Yet with all the attention it receives, peace never seems to be found.

There are two basic forms of peace that truly matter. The Bible speaks of these as the peace *with* God and the peace *of* God.

Peace *with* God is granted when a person believes and receives Jesus Christ as Savior. Romans 5:1 explains: "Therefore, since we have been justified through faith, we have peace with God through our Lord Jesus Christ."

This kind of peace is "positional" in nature. Being in Christ, we are no longer at enmity with God; we have peace with Him and are not faced with the prospect of His wrath. Our spiritual position assures our eternal peace.

The other kind of peace—the peace *of* God—is not positional, but practical. Paul spoke of this peace to the Philippians: "Do not be anxious about anything, but in everything, by prayer and petition, with thanksgiving, present your requests to God. And the peace of God, which transcends all understanding, will guard your hearts and your minds in Christ Jesus" (4:6,7).

This kind of peace is not passivity. It is not the absence of conflict. It is the quietness of heart and mind that comes when we know that Christ is in control of everything—even the things that cause us anxiety.

Peace is not the result of good self-image, a balanced bank account, or a high social standing. Peace is found only in a Person.

The peace of God is like a sentinel, set to guard our souls from all that would disturb or destroy. It takes up its position as a direct result of our deliberate submission of everything to God in prayer. Without prayer there can be no peace. With prayer there is a calmness and quietness, whatever the situation.

This life will always be full of trouble, even for the believer. Our faith does not exempt us from the struggles of being human. We will always face circumstances that could cause us to fear. Doubt and anxiety are constantly trying to work their way into our souls. But we have a resource for coping with our trials that the world knows nothing about. Jesus said to His disciples, "I have told you these things so that in me you may have peace. In this world you will have trouble. But take heart! I have overcome the world" (John 16:33).

"In me you may have peace."

There is the secret. Peace is not found in self-help books or psychiatric therapy. It is not the result of good self-image, a balanced bank account, or a high social standing. Peace is found only in a Person, the Lord Jesus Christ. He alone is the Prince of Peace, and He longs to rule in your heart.

If they had only known that truth, 67 scholars from 19 countries could have saved themselves a lot of time.

44

Pearls

Overcoming Difficulties

If there is one thing certain in life it is this: We shall all meet up with trouble. Trouble comes to everyone from the white-collar millionaire to the hobo on the street.

There are all kinds of trouble. Troubles of the soul, mind, and body. Troubles that we bring upon ourselves through neglect or sin. Troubles that others bring upon us. Troubles that have a logical reason and troubles that have no reason at all.

Recently a lady came to my office who was experiencing a large dose of trouble in her family. Her husband's salary had been cut in half due to problems within his company, her daughter had become a major problem in the family, and she was facing surgery in the near future. As we discussed these problems I shared with her three things that would aid her in her quest to overcome her difficulties.

First, if we are Christians, God allows the trouble that comes our way. We cannot say that God brings our troubles upon us, because God is a holy, compassionate, loving God, but we can rest assured that He often does allow the trouble that comes. Many times He must do this in order to bring us back to the place of humility and willingness where we need to be.

I'm reminded of the prophet Jonah, who had to be placed in the belly of a fish before he would submit to God's will. God certainly had a good reason for allowing trouble to come into his life, and if you are a Christian you can know that He has an equally good reason for allowing the troubles that come your way.

Second, when we find ourselves in trouble we should call upon God for help. In Psalm 50 God tells us, "Call upon Me in the day of trouble; I will deliver you, and you shall glorify me" (verse 15 NKJV). How do we call upon God? We call through prayer. Prayer for the troubled soul is what a lifeline is to a drowning man.

Third, we must realize the good that comes from our troubles. David said, "It was good for me to be afflicted" (Psalm 119:71). I know that this is a difficult admission to make. It has been in my life. When in the midst of troubles we ask, "What good could possibly come out of this mess?" But when it is over we can always look back and see the good we have gained. Trust in God, and sympathy for those who are encountering a similar situation, are only a few lessons that come to those who have traveled the troubled path.

A Christian's response to trouble can be illustrated by the oyster who awakens one morning to find that a discomforting grain of sand has slipped into his shell during the night. What shall the oyster do? Well, there are several paths he could take. The oyster could determine to block the problem entirely out of his mind, convincing himself that the grain of sand just isn't there, boring and cutting into his skin.

But the oyster doesn't do that, for this attitude would soon collapse under the weight of his pain. Again the oyster could look up to God and say, "Why did this happen to me? Why with all the millions of other oysters in the ocean did You pick on me? What did I ever do to deserve this?" Yes, the oyster could say that, like so many of us do when trouble comes.

But he doesn't. No, the oyster has learned a better way of dealing with his trouble. Ever so carefully he begins to cover the grain of sand with a milky coating. Time and time again the rough edges are covered, until that troublesome grain of sand has miraculously become a pearl of great price. An uncomfortable intruder has been turned into a gem.

Let us learn a lesson from this fact of nature: God is willing and able to help us turn our troubles into the pearls of our life.

45

Perfection

Removing Guilt and Condemnation

No matter how hard we try, we all fall short of this illusive thing called perfection. There is not a person alive who hasn't made some serious mistakes that he wishes he could erase from his life. No matter how good our intentions may be, we often fail to perform to the level of those expectations. Wrong attitudes, harsh words, bitter reactions, and painful responses all add up to produce a load of guilt that we cannot seem to unload by ourselves.

I wish I could tell you that life can be lived in perfection. I wish I could assure you that you will never be tempted again in this world. I wish I could emphatically declare that you will never make another mistake as long as you live, but that is just not the way life is. The Bible reminds us, "For all have sinned, and come short of the glory of God" (Romans 3:23 KJV).

We are constantly reminded of our fallibility every time we make a mistake. Whether it is a minor glitch or a tragic error, we all need forgiveness for our sins. In fact, we not only need a Savior to forgive our mistakes, but we need Someone to remove our guilt and condemnation as well.

During World War II, a chaplain came across a young soldier dying on a battlefield. He took him up gently in his arms and said, "Son, you don't have long to live. Is there anything I can do for you?"

As he was dying, the young man's life flashed before his mind. He recalled the sins of his youth and the many times he had broken his parents' hearts with his rebellious living. He remembered the times he had turned his back on God and denied the voice of conviction in his soul.

As he looked up into the chaplain's face the soldier sighed, "No, sir, there is nothing you can do for me. I need somebody who can undo some things for me."

Charles Spurgeon, the famous Baptist pastor of the nineteenth century, said, "Sin is a knot only God can untie." Sometimes our mistakes are such that they leave our lives in a tangled mess. Sin complicates every aspect of life. It will destroy your health, incriminate your behavior, besmirch your character, eliminate your future, and shorten your life.

But despite our failures and mistakes, there is good news for every person: *Christ loves us enough to forgive our sins, to remove our guilt, and to cleanse us from all unrighteousness.* There is not a single person whom our Lord will not forgive if he will but repent and seek His forgiveness. Jesus is willing to cleanse, renew, and restore if we only ask. Perfection is reachable, but only as we are found in Christ. For perfection belongs to Him and Him alone.

46

Power

Comfort for the Heart

I often wonder how God views the human race. There must be ten thousand different ways—perhaps even as many as there are people on this earth. As I think on this I am reminded of the Bible's statement that "He who sits in the heavens shall laugh" (Psalm 2:4 NKJV). I am inclined to believe that this refers to some divine amusement that God must have over the boastful attitudes and works of men. Men who state, for example, "God is dead." Men who blaspheme Him in word and deed. Men who time after time in raw confidence oppose the living God, showing nothing but insult for their Creator while they wallow in their futile blankets of security.

Belshazzar the king of Babylon was just such a man. The prophet Daniel tells us of the arrogance and self-security of this ancient king—how he had prepared a feast for a thousand of his lords and their ladies to drink and dance, defying the God of Israel. But why not? He was the king of Babylon, the greatest city in the known world.

When we read the report of Herodotus we can understand why Belshazzar felt so secure in his challenge to God. Babylon was a city unparalleled in the history of this world.

It measured 15 miles square and 60 miles in circumference. The outside walls were 350 feet high, 700 feet wide at the bottom, and 300 feet wide at the top. Seven chariots could race around the top of these walls side by side. Then there were the inner walls. On top of these walls, which stood 250 feet high, was a standing army kept ready night and day to pour caldrons of hot melted lead on the heads of any invading army. The city had 25 streets running north, south, east, and west, with each city block 2/3 of a mile square.

At the center of the city sat the temple of the pagan god Baal. It rested on 150 pillars standing 88 feet in the air. Hewn from solid marble, it housed a 40-foot image of the pagan sun god covered in solid gold. Nearby, in the city square, was the palace of Belshazzar the king. It is in the ballroom that we are interested, because that is where God paid His unexpected visit. This ballroom was 1,650 feet wide and over a mile long. Seventeen football fields could be placed end to end in the massive room. About 4500 pillars in the form of huge elephants were part of those walls, and upon their backs sat bronze gladiators which towered another 125 feet in the air.

From the hand of each gladiator swung a chain across the expanse of the room. When woven together these formed a golden net upon which hung the famous Hanging Gardens of Babylon. Each dining table was made in the form of a horseshoe, so that each lord and his ladies could gather while trained peacocks drew chariots of fine wines and choice meats from table to table. Coming from the garden was the music of the King's Orchestra, composed of around 32,000 musicians.

What a city! It is easy to understand how Belshazzar could boast of his security even in the face of God. He thought he had the world in the palm of his hand, but little did he know that soon he would die.

Like Belshazzar, man after man will come and go, and nations will rise and fall, each one standing boldly to oppose God, but always the record will be the same: "It is a fearful thing to fall into the hands of the living God!"

The awesome power of our God is unmatched by human hands. And to think that this power also watches over and protects God's children, and we are those children!

Second Chronicles 16:9 reminds us that "the eyes of the Lord run to and fro throughout the whole earth, to show Himself strong on behalf of those whose heart is loyal to Him" (NKJV).

Let your heart be comforted by that truth today.

47

Praise

Recognizing God's Sovereignty

Habakkuk penned his prophecy in a time of growing uncertainty. The good King Josiah had died and Judah was suffering under rebellious King Johoiakim. Violence, perversion, and injustice were everywhere—much like this morning's headlines in *USA Today*.

Habakkuk saw the wickedness in his own people. His heart grieved over their sin. He knew that judgment hovered in the air. He wondered how Judah would respond when God brought the Babylonians in to do His work. How would the people react when the reckoning began? Out of his heart he wrote:

Though the fig tree does not bud
and there are no grapes on the vines,
though the olive crop fails
and the fields produce no food,
though there are no sheep in the pen
and no cattle in the stalls,
yet I will rejoice in the LORD,
I will be joyful in God my Savior.
The Sovereign LORD is my strength.

—Habakkuk 3:17-19

Habakkuk looked into the future and saw the coming famine and destruction. But he also saw his sovereign God in these events. Knowing that God was still his Savior and Lord, He was able to rejoice. Whatever was to come, his heart was fixed: He would trust and be joyful in God because He had not changed.

This is the definition of true praise: *recognizing God for who He is.* Praise is that fountain of adoration and worship that springs up in the heart of the believer when he catches a glimpse of the nature and character of God.

True praise is not determined by any circumstance—good or bad, positive or negative, helpful or harmful. Praise is about God and God alone—His majesty, His glory, His holiness, His power and strength. Praise is simply telling God what He is like. It is rehearsing in His ears the beauties and glories you see in Him, the things about Him that delight you and fill you with wonder. Praise is adding your voice to the song of the stars and the unheard music of the angels who celebrate His awesomeness. It is first and foremost a private matter of the heart, though it can be shared publicly as well.

But all true praise has an audience of one: Almighty God. It is directed to Him alone. It is about Him. It is for Him. It must arise out of reverence and godly fear, out of a heart that has been cleansed and made pure.

Genuine, worshipful praise has been missing from the life of the church for many years. Its rediscovery has done much for us all. It is as if the church is seeing God again in all His glory.

Praise is a wonderful thing. God does inhabit the praises of His people. But much of what passes for praise today is little more than spiritual cheerleading—wild celebrations when points are scored and desperate urgings to performance when we think we are in danger of losing.

But God cannot be manipulated, *even by our praise*. He is Sovereign. He is Lord. We praise Him because of who He is, not because of what He gives us. *He Himself* is the object of our adoration, and not the blessings He gives. He is the One we celebrate and appreciate, not for what He will do for us in return, but simply because He is. The real idea behind praise is not that it benefits us at all, but that it glorifies the Father.

Habakkuk knew this. His country faced deserved judgment, and soon women and children would be suffering starvation. Husbands and fathers would be killed or taken captive. Judah would be overrun by the cruel, arrogant Babylonians.

Suffering loomed. Grim days lay ahead. Many people would forget God or blame Him for their trouble. But not Habakkuk. He had already settled in his heart that he would rejoice in God. In the face of calamity and even death, he would exalt Him. This would not change his circumstance, nor would it alter what God had purposed, but it would give God what belonged to Him: worship, submission, and praise.

Oh, for a heart that is fixed on God *no matter what happens*. Oh, for a devotion to Him that is steadfast, for lips that will praise His unchanging love and faithfulness, though all the world crumbles around our feet! This is the praise that pleases the Father and brings glory to His name.

48

Prayer

Daily Communion

Have you ever had days that pass when you haven't taken time to pray? Then, when you do begin your prayer life, your prayers seem to bounce right back at you? I know I have, and most Christians would have to admit to the same. But isn't it wonderful that when your prayer life is straightened out, the other things that caused irritation seem to fall into place. Your life, home, family, and job all run smoothly because your heart is in one accord with God.

Often it is difficult for us to learn that true prayer is not an "up-and-down," "on-and-off" process. Continued prayer must be the practice of our lives if we are to learn the secret of Acts 6:4: "We will give ourselves continually to prayer" (NKJV).

As children, when we wanted or needed something, we went to our parents or the one in authority and asked for it. Of course, the answer was one of three things: yes, no, or wait. This seems to be the way God answers our prayers also. Some things that we ask of God cannot be answered with a yes, no matter how much we desire them. Furthermore, if we do not receive this much-wanted yes to our petition, we must not think that this is always a no. Perhaps God wants us to wait for something better. If so, during this time we must continue in prayer as the disciples did.

Luke records that Jesus went up on a mountain to pray and remained there all night in prayer. Scripture neither records His prayer nor gives the nature of it, but in the very next verse we see Jesus choosing His disciples. In all our decisions we need God's guidance, even as Jesus asked His Father's guidance in the selection of these 12 men.

Yes, continued prayer must be part of each Christian's life. God doesn't automatically give to us because there is a need, but He expects us to ask of Him. James tells us that we have not because we ask not. We must ask, not taking it for granted that God mechanically supplies our wants and needs.

Daily communion with God draws us closer to Him, helps us along life's way, and helps our faith and spiritual strength to grow.

God is not asleep or dead,
As some would have me say.
You see, I know he's living still,
For I talked to Him today.

—Author unknown

Talk with God. He is listening for your prayer today!

49

Rest

Pausing for Everlasting Love

Ours is a restless world. Everyone is on the go and in a great hurry. Have you dared the freeways lately? How about your neighborhood street? Is it just me, or is everyone driving faster these days? If people are not rocketing down the concrete strips of our cities, they are jogging alongside them, headphones in place, their faces a mask of intense concentration.

We all have too much to do and too little time to do it in. So we eat on the run, pick up our kids on the run, and do errands on the run. We run, run, run and still don't get done, done, done.

But it's not the physical pace alone. Just beneath the surface of our hectic lives, worry and fear gnaw at our security and peace of mind. We are concerned about the state of the world, the balance in our checking account, the well-being of our kids, the security of our jobs, and the prospects for our future. We are overwhelmed intellectually and emotionally by each day's requirements. Most of us go to bed at night unable to relax our exhausted bodies because our minds will not stop racing.

To the frantic soul caught up in our twentieth-century pace of life comes Jesus' welcome, age-old invitation: "Come to Me, all you who labor and are heavy laden, and I will give you rest" (Matthew 11:28 NKJV).

Rest.

Remember what that means?

It's that hammock under the tree in the summer . . . the sun-drenched sand and salt spray on the beach . . . that fluffy, overstuffed chair by the window.

Relaxation. Repose. A pause.

The first mention of the word "rest" in the Bible refers to God. After He created the universe and everything in it, He rested on the seventh day. He pushed back from His works. He looked at them, and He saw that they were finished and that they were good. So He rested. Hebrews tells us there is also a rest for the people of God. One secret of entering that rest is found in those two little words that characterized God's rest: "finished" and "good."

We can rest, as God did, because of a finished work.

Once we realize we have a full, complete salvation, that God will complete the work He began in us, that everything which comes to us in life comes couched in God's love—amazingly, the emotional and spiritual exhaustion is gone.

Solomon said, "I know that whatever God does, it shall be forever. Nothing can be added to it, and nothing taken from it" (Ecclesiastes 3:14 NKJV). Our eternal salvation is God's work, and it was finished at the cross. He needs to do nothing else. We don't have to meet any more standards to be accepted by Him. Salvation has been won. And what He began in us He will carry on to completion (Philippians 1:6). We are His workmanship (Ephesians 2:10). He will perfect everything that concerns us (Psalm 138:8 NKJV). He is both the Author and the Finisher of our faith.

Something else characterized that initial rest of God: It was a good work.

Behind so much of our earnest activity is the hidden fear that somehow God has less than our best interests at heart. We suffer from a distorted picture of Him, as if He were a father who would give us a stone when we really need bread. No wonder we find it hard to trust Him. How we need to grow in our understanding of the character of God!

He is *good.*

Everything He does is *good.*

He can do nothing else.

The thoughts He thinks toward us are thoughts of peace, not of evil (Jeremiah 29:11 NKJV). He loves us with an everlasting love, tender as a mother's, strong as a father's. We need never fear anything that comes from His hand, for it will result in good (Romans 8:28). We don't have to watch out anxiously for our own welfare. He cares for us and He is good.

In the final analysis, most of the frantic lifestyle that characterizes our day is a cover-up, an attempt to avoid the real, spiritual insecurities that weigh on our hearts and minds. Another reason many of us are frantic is because or wrong or misplaced priorities. Once we realize we have a full, complete salvation, that God will complete the work He began in us, that everything which comes to us in life comes couched in God's love—amazingly, the emotional and spiritual exhaustion is gone.

We can find rest in the midst of our hectic activities—not in our own works, but in His.

They are finished.

And they are good.

50

Restoration

Mending Lives

Antiques lovingly restored.

The sign stood outside the little shop in north Georgia. Inside was a jumble of old appliances, jewelry, clothing, dishes, and pieces of furniture in varying stages of disrepair.

"Many of these items are one-of-a-kind," said the lady tending shop.

I nodded, running my hand over the dark, pitted surface of an oak headboard.

"The workmanship and materials can never be replaced," she went on. "Solid wood. Real silver. But just because some of these things are old . . . just because of the normal wear and tear of good, useful service—folks throw 'em out. Say they're undesirable.

"These have all been discarded," she continued, gesturing at the items that crowded the little showroom. "The owners wanted something new. Breaks my heart. Just a little repair, a little wax, a few stitches here and there, and you'd have something really valuable. It's a real shame . . . it seems we've lost the art of mending, and we're the poorer for it."

Her words echoed in my mind for days to come.

"We've lost the art of mending. . . ."

She was talking about furniture and clothing. Pieces of wood, hunks of metal, strips of fabric. Stuff. Things. But I thought of the broken lives I've seen through the years, lives in desperate need of mending. They were like the castoffs in her store: many of them well-worn from service for the Lord. Many scarred by hard experiences. Stained. Nicked and scratched by rough treatment at the hands of others. Some of them had even fallen apart through their own mistakes.

How many of them had received the loving care they needed?

How many of them had been neglected—put off for lack of concern or lack of time?

How many had been used and then rejected?

How many had been shunned for years as damaged goods?

How many dumped for something new?

How many written off as out-of-date?

Restoration takes time. There has to be a stripping away of the old, the torn, and the ruined before the new can be applied. It can't be rushed. And it takes a gentle and careful touch. Every item has its process and every part of the process has its place. What works for a piece of furniture would be devastating to a silk shawl. Sometimes you have to use strong chemicals, sometimes tiny tools. It takes intimate knowledge of the item and a knowing and patient hand to do it right.

God is in the restoration business. To the nation of Israel He said, "I will restore health to you and heal you of your wounds . . . because they called you an outcast, saying, 'This is Zion; no one seeks her'" (Jeremiah 30:17 NKJV).

Through His prophet Joel He promised, "I will restore to you the years that the swarming locust has eaten. . . . You shall eat in plenty and be satisfied, and praise the name of the Lord your God . . . and My people shall never be put to shame" (Joel 2:25,26 NKJV).

God specializes in taking lives that are broken and scarred and cast off and making them new. He knows exactly what is needed, and He applies it gently and carefully. He never uses the wrong tools. He never uses the wrong process or the wrong amount of pressure.

His restoration is perfect.

He wants His church to do the same. Galatians tells us that we should restore those brothers who have been overtaken by sin. The word "restore" is the same word "mend" used in the New Testament to describe James and John mending their nets.

God wants us to mend each other. To repair and restore each other to wholeness and beauty and usefulness. Just like He does for each of us.

Unfortunately, we more often judge and destroy one another. It has been said that the Christian church is the only army in the world that shoots its own wounded. How tragic that friendly fire should finish off the weak, the weary, and the maimed! How tragic that judgment and neglect should characterize a people so wholly forgiven and restored by their God!

How tragic that we have lost our Father's art of mending men and women.

We need to serve a new apprenticeship in our Father's

restoration shop, watching His skilled hands and loving heart remove stains, strip away the years of neglect, and draw deep beauty and utility out of used and rejected lives.

He is willing to train us if we are willing to learn.

He would love nothing more.

After all, restoration is a family business.

51

Secure

Our True Source of Stability

Peppermint Patty once asked Charlie Brown to define security. His reply was priceless.

"Security? Security is sleeping in the backseat of the car. When you're a little kid, and you've been somewhere with your mom and dad, and it's night, and you're riding home in the car, you can sleep in the backseat. You don't have to worry about anything. Your mom and dad are in the front seat, and do all the worrying. They take care of everything."[9]

Do you remember that wonderful part of being a child? Of not having to worry about anything because you had a mom and dad who took care of you? You probably never gave a thought to where your next meal would come from. You just showed up at the regular time and there it was. You probably never imagined not having a roof over your head or clothes to wear. You had a mom and dad. They took care of those things.

Charlie Brown knew he was secure because of who his parents were. His comfort and peace were tied to the character and performance of that couple in the front seat. His experiences with them had led him to believe and trust in their ability to keep him safe . . . to get him home and into his pajamas and his own bed. He knew he could trust them.

And so it is with us. Our security is tied to the Person God is. If He is not trustworthy, all is lost; the backseat becomes a place of fear and dread, not a haven and a refuge. Who is this God? What is it about Him that gives us confidence, that makes us feel safe? What do we know about Him that proves His trustworthiness?

First of all, we know He cannot lie. The book of Numbers tells us, "God is not a man, that He should lie, nor a son of man, that He should repent. Has He said, and will He not do it? Or has He spoken, and will He not make it good?" (Numbers 23:19 NKJV).

God keeps His Word. Period.

Jesus said not one dot of an *i* or cross of a *t* would fail until every word of God had been fulfilled. The psalmist reminds us that His words are very sure, that they have been tested and tried and have been found to be pure and utterly trustworthy.

What a source of stability this is for us! In the world, millions of words are spoken each day, and very few of them count for anything. Promises are easily made and easily broken. Contracts and vows are routinely cast aside as situations change. Even sacred vows of marriage are jettisoned as a matter of convenience. Sometimes in our cynicism and despair it seems that *no one's* word is good.

But God's Word is different. He doesn't lie. He *cannot* lie. What He promised, *He will perform.* We need never doubt what He said. It is sure.

We also know that He never changes. "I am the Lord; I change not," He declared through His prophet. Jesus Christ is the same yesterday, today, and forever. What He purposed in ages past He purposes today. His kingdom is unshakable. No geopolitical upheavals or plans of man will ever change it. It is built upon a foundation, a tested cornerstone.

His utterly truthful, unchanging character is what gives us security. Listen to the writer of Hebrews:

> Because God wanted to make the unchanging nature of his purpose very clear to the heirs of what was promised, he confirmed it with an oath. God did this so that, by two unchangeable things in which it is impossible for God to lie, we who have fled to take hold of the hope offered to us may be greatly encouraged. We have this hope as an anchor for the soul, firm and secure (Hebrews 6:17-19).

God knows the propensity of our hearts to doubt. He knows our struggle in a world of uncertainty and constant change. He knows our need for an anchor in life, a firm grounding in the shifting tide of restless waves. He offers us His Word and His character as guarantees of His purpose. He wants us to know with assurance that we are safe and secure in Him.

Charlie Brown was right. Security can be found in the backseat . . . when the one in the front seat is someone as utterly truthful and trustworthy as God.

52

Self

Winning Internal Battles

There is an ancient Greek legend that tells of a young man who was haunted in his dreams by a strange veiled figure. Each time he was about to gain peace and joy, this veiled figure would come out of the darkness, attack his mind and bring anxiety and fear. When about to gain fame and fortune, the villain would rob him of his riches and ruin his reputation. Each thing he attempted to do in life turned into a complete failure because of the unknown oppressor. Finally, when he could stand it no more, the enraged young man cried out, "Who are you?" and stretching forth his hand ripped the veil from his tormentor's face. Astonished, he screamed in fear, for the face he beheld was his own.

A great truth lies within this story: People can bring success or ruin upon themselves. People can become their own number one enemy.

In Bible times the greatest heroes were those who could win the battle. Many times the Bible records the story of some great general who led his army into battle, defeating the enemy, subduing the land, and taking the cities of his foe. Upon returning home the general would be greeted by praise and fanfare as the people paid respect to their leader who had captured the prize of all prizes—the city of his foe. But the Scriptures go on to say that there is a far greater victory than this: "He that ruleth his own spirit is greater than he that taketh a city" (from Proverbs 16:32 KJV). The greatest battle a person must fight is not from without, but from within. It is a battle against jealousy, temperament, lust, and a multitude of other evil forces that each person, with the help of God, must overcome by himself.

Perhaps you feel that life has dealt you a raw deal. Nothing seems to go right; everybody and everything seems to be wrong. If so, why not tear the veil from your tormentor's face? Acknowledge your shortcomings and ask God to forgive you, help you, and give you peace.

53

Simplicity

Singleness of the Soul

In the late 1800s a young lady went to church in Chicago to hear the man her mother called the greatest preacher in America. Upon returning home, the girl told her mother that this Dwight L. Moody could not possibly be considered a great preacher.

"Why not?" asked her mother.

"Because," replied the girl, "I understood everything he had to say."

Though this story occurred before the turn of the century, it reflects what has become a mindset today: If it's simple, it can't be important. The explosion of scientific discovery and technology in recent decades has convinced us that if something isn't complex and mind-boggling in its intricacy, it has no significance. It seems the more elaborate and sophisticated the object or its process, the better it must be.

We spend hundreds of dollars on machines designed to make life easier and more convenient, only to find that the directions defy understanding. You almost need an engineering degree to program your microwave or VCR! Whatever happened to making simple household repairs or working on your own car in the garage? Have you tried to buy an ordinary typewriter lately—one that didn't check your grammar and your blood pressure and do 50 other things? What about a sewing machine for a beginning seamstress? Everything is computerized nowadays; the simple machines of even a few years ago are found only in second-hand shops and antique stores.

> The simple life, according to the Word, is a matter of the heart. It is a life that is holy—a life that has been reduced to desiring righteousness alone, uncomplicated by sin and deception.

Many would say the idea of simplicity doesn't belong in this advanced age—the age of reason, of science, of technology. The person who longs for more uncomplicated ways of life is seen as intellectually weak, unable to cope with the demands of a fast-paced, ever-changing world. But Oscar Wilde said it best: "Life is not complex. *We* are complex."

The complexity we need to fear and lament is not that of machines, but that of the human heart.

The Bible uses the word "simplicity" to mean purity, sincerity, and generosity. It has to do with singleness of the soul. Matthew 6:22 uses the same word for the "single" eye that determines the quality of our life: "If thine eye is single, thy whole body shall be full of light" (from KJV).

You see, life ceases to be complex when it is properly focused. The simple life, according to the Word, is a matter of the heart. It is a life that is holy—a life that has been reduced to desiring righteousness alone, uncomplicated by sin and deception. It is the heart of John Huss, who from the martyr's stake cried out, *"O sancta simplicatas!"*. . . "O holy simplicity!"

Paul feared that the Corinthians' minds would be drawn away from the "simplicity that is in Christ" (2 Corinthians 11:3 NKJV). He knew the true complexities to be avoided—the deception, dishonesty, and duplicity of sin. The gospel message is so powerful because it is so beautifully simple. It isn't hard for anyone to understand—it's just hard for some to believe.

Recently I had the opportunity to tell a young man about how Christ could take the sin from his life and bring him peace. At first he would not accept Christ's way of salvation.

"It's too simple," he told me.

But after we talked on, he came to see that this was one of the beauties of God's plan. It is complex enough that all the universe is astounded at the event, but simple enough for us all to partake in it, making it possible for both the university professor and the child in school to have this wonderful gift of salvation.

Next time you feel that life is getting too complex, too harried, too impersonal . . . check your eyes. Are they seeing double—focusing on the world, on your personal concerns, on your goals, on your worries or fears? Or are they single—focused on Christ and pleasing Him?

Holiness is, after all, the simplest way to go.

54

Today

Reflecting Christ

The following pledge that I wrote some time ago has been a valuable aid to my daily outlook; I thought I might share it with you.

Today I will live moment by moment. I will not allow my mind to linger on yesterday nor dwell too long upon tomorrow.

Today to the best of my ability I will follow some schedule in order to make the best use of my time. I will remind myself that time is the most valuable thing I can spend.

Today I will begin with the reading of God's Word and morning prayer with the One who will direct my thoughts and actions throughout the coming hours.

Today I will dress as neatly as possible and have a clean appearance so that others will find me physically pleasant to be around.

Today I will greet everyone I meet with a smile, for this is perhaps the only thing I will be able to give them that they do not already have. I will purpose in my heart not to speak unkindly to anyone, especially my enemies, while I guard my heart from jealousy, hatred, lust, and a thousand other vices that are waiting to overcome me.

Today I will keep my mind from negative thoughts, speak optimistically to a pessimistic friend, attempt something that I have always felt was impossible, and set a new goal that I might aim to reach.

Today I will not be overly critical of the opinion of others, but will stand for those things in which I believe without fear of anyone who might challenge or contradict them.

Today I will spend time in mental and physical exercise, having the knowledge that an alert mind and strong body are both essential in completing the tasks which are set before me. I will not allow myself to become a loafer of any degree.

Today I will spend time with my family. I will do my best to express to my wife in both word and deed the love I have for her. I shall hold my children and tell them of something beautiful in order to plant a seed of inspiration in their hearts. I will attempt to live such a life before them that these seeds of goodness may be watered by kindness and love. I shall be honest with them. Even though I may not be perfect, they shall know me for what I am.

At the end of this day, when its tasks are completed, I will lie down to rest with the confidence that when another day comes I shall arise with a new verse in my heart: "This is the day which the Lord has made; we will rejoice and be glad in it" (Psalm 118:24).

55

Tomorrow

Time Filtered by God

We humans are strange creatures.

It seems we can't get our sense of timing right. We're prone to get out of step with what God has said about time and the way we view it.

Though He Himself is timeless, He knows our frame of reference is bound by *yesterdays, todays*, and *tomorrows*. He knows how we struggle with them, how we mishandle them. We spend our lives regretting the past, complaining about the present, and worrying about the future.

And so He speaks to us about all of these.

The *yesterdays* with their mistakes and regrets and sorrows.

The *todays* with their struggles and needs.

The *tomorrows* with their possibilities and dangers.

His word to us about the past is to both remember and forget. Remember God's wise and gracious kindness to you through the years, and forget those empty days when you wandered from Him and stumbled, wounding yourself and others. That past cannot be changed. It is gone.

And He tells us how to handle the present: one day at a time.

But some of His most striking comments have to do with our attitude toward the future.

His first word to us is, *Don't count on tomorrow. It may not happen as you've planned.* Proverbs 27:1 warns us that we shouldn't boast about tomorrow because we really don't know what it may bring forth. James speaks directly to the busy executives with their five-year plans detailed in leatherbound time-management books.

> Just a moment, now, you who say, "We are going to such-and-such a city today or tomorrow. We shall stay there a year doing business and make a profit! How do you know what will happen tomorrow? What, after all, is your life? It is like a puff of smoke visible for a little while and then dissolving into thin air. Your remarks should be prefaced with, "If it is the Lord's will, we shall still be alive and will do so-and-so." As it is, you take a certain pride in planning with such confidence. That sort of pride is all wrong (James 4:13-16, PHILLIPS).

Though it isn't wrong to have a plan for the future, it is wrong to have a plan that doesn't take God's will into account. Setting a course for your life without the direction of God is nothing more than boasting and bragging. And God says it is all wrong; it is evil.

Then He says, *Don't dread tomorrow—it will take care of itself.* In the Sermon on the Mount, Jesus spoke to those who looked to the future with dread and apprehension. They were fearful that they wouldn't have enough to eat or to wear. Worry was their constant companion. Reminding them that they had a heavenly Father who knew all about their needs and was more than adequate to meet them, Jesus plainly said, Do not worry about tomorrow, for tomorrow will worry about itself. Each day has enough trouble of its own (Matthew 6:34). And it follows that each day also has enough grace for its needs, but the grace, like the trouble, is given one day at a time.

Then He says *not to ignore tomorrow for it has a direct effect on how we live today.* There is much we do not know about the future. However, we do know that there is a tomorrow that will usher in eternity. There will be a tomorrow when we meet the Lord in the air and go to be with Him forever. There will be a tomorrow when all that we know as earth and heaven will be recreated, when sin and Satan will finally be destroyed. Peter brings that tomorrow into proper focus in one of his final admonitions.

> Therefore, since all these things will be dissolved, what manner of persons ought you to be in holy conduct and godliness, looking for and hastening the coming of the day of God, because of which the heavens will be dissolved being on fire, and the elements will melt with fervent heat? Nevertheless we, according to His promise, look for new heavens and a new earth in which righteousness dwells. Therefore, beloved, looking forward to these things, be diligent to be found by Him in peace, without spot and blameless (2 Peter 3:11-14).

God gave us this hope of tomorrow that our today might be used for His honor and glory. It is a purifying hope, an anticipation that should result in a life of greater consecration to Him.

Tomorrow. Don't count on it egotistically and don't dread it fearfully, but don't ignore it apathetically, either. God is the God of all our days. And like a good shepherd who goes before his sheep and knows what lies ahead, He filters every tomorrow through His love, His goodness, His faithfulness. We need never be afraid when we trust an unknown future into the hands of our all-knowing God.

56

Touch

The Human Connection

He had known only loneliness for so long.

How many years since he had seen his family? Three? Five? How long since he had shared a meal with them, laughing and planning and hoping for tomorrow? How long since he had put his hands to an honest day's work? How long since he had watched a setting sun, feeling he had accomplished something?

How long?

Then there was the ugliness. His fingers were growing white and disappearing with the ravages of his disease. His face was already disfigured. The disease was not just taking his body, it was eating away his very humanity. He was no longer whole. He was only a caricature of the man he had been.

So it didn't take him long to decide. Risking the anger and humiliation of public exposure, he ran to Jesus, fell at His feet, and cried, "Lord, if you are willing, you can make me clean!"

He held his breath. Would Jesus be willing? Would He heal him and return him to the land of the living . . . to family and friends and work and love and joy and life itself?

He had the slimmest of hopes that Jesus might speak a word to him. What Jesus actually did went beyond hope.

He touched him.

Moved with compassion, Jesus stretched out His hand and touched the untouchable leper. Then He spoke the words, "I am willing; be clean." And immediately the leprosy was gone!

Have you ever wondered why Jesus touched this man? Many people He healed with merely the spoken word, but this man He touched. Why? *Because he needed it.* This unidentified leper hadn't been touched by anyone in years. His spirit was starved for a human connection. Jesus knew the emotional cost of his physical suffering . . . the isolation and loneliness. He touched the leper to let him know he was no longer alone.

We are just beginning to understand all that is bound up in the human touch, how vital it is to good health, both physically and emotionally. There seems to be a deep psychological and spiritual need for all that it communicates.

Pain isolates. It makes us withdraw from our surroundings. We become blinded to what is around us. But the touch of another human being is a lifeline. There are times when nothing ministers like that affirming touch on the shoulder or the grasp of the hand that says, "I'm here with you. I know you're hurting, and I'm here." When a touch is needed, nothing else will do to break down walls or heal hurts. When inappropriate and unnecessary, though, a touch can do much harm. It takes the sensitivity of the Spirit to know what is needed and the touch of Christ to supply it.

Jesus knew those who needed to be touched. And He never hesitated to reach out to them, no matter how untouchable they seemed to be.

Look around you today. Who is hurting? Who is withering under the isolation and pain of hard times? Who is holding his breath, desperate for the affirmation and strength of a human touch?

Be the hands of Jesus today. Let Him touch the wounded through you and thereby minister His love and healing grace.

57

Transformed

The Ultimate Metamorphosis

"Be transformed by the renewing of your mind" (Romans 12:2).

The word *transformed* translates the term *metamorphosis* in the original Greek. It implies a basic change in the Christian's inward nature and results in a brand-new pattern of character and behavior that corresponds to our new nature in Christ. This transformation is such a drastic change that it alters our entire being.

Metamorphosis is the term used to describe the transformation of a caterpillar into a butterfly. Have you ever observed a caterpillar crawling along the sidewalk? It isn't a pleasant sight. It is slimy, fuzzy, and squishy, but eventually it spins itself into a cocoon. Even the cocoon isn't pleasant to see. But inside that gray little incubator an incredible transformation is taking place. Finally the cocoon breaks open and a beautiful butterfly emerges with all the striking colors that nature can give it.

The transformation of a caterpillar into a butterfly is so drastic that it is hard to believe the butterfly was ever a caterpillar. Yet a similar incredible process occurs by the life-changing power of God's grace. The Bible states it like this: "Therefore if any man be in Christ, he is a new creature; old things are passed away; behold, all things are become new" (2 Corinthians 5:17 KJV).

When you and I come to the end of ourselves, we stop trying to make ourselves better by our own self-effort. Only when we are willing to abandon the philosophies of this world and surrender to the will of God can we ever find true meaning and happiness in life. When we stop working, God begins to work. When we start trusting, He starts transforming. The evangelist Charles Spurgeon said it, and it is true: "We cannot always trace God's hand, but we can always trust God's heart."

58

Truth

The Framework of Freedom

A Welsh miner came to Dr. Paul Brand one day, needing surgery. The miner had lost the bone of his upper arm many years before due to a tumor. The bone had been surgically removed, leaving the skin and muscles hanging loosely in place.

Though his lower arm was completely healthy, the miner could not use it. Whenever he attempted to, the upper arm muscles contracted helplessly, much like an earthworm does when touched. Without the bone, the muscles were useless and motion was restricted. His doctor, however, had fitted him with an ingenious metal brace that could be strapped around the upper arm to mimic the function of the missing internal bone. Whenever he wanted to raise his arm, the metal literally braced his biceps, keeping them from drawing up and allowing the proper force to be exerted to raise his lower arm. In reality it functioned as an outer bone, allowing the movement he could otherwise not enjoy.

Dr. Brand compares the bones of our skeleton to the fundamental truths of our Christian faith. Both are a framework that results in freedom. He states:

> The 206 lengths of calcium our body is strapped to are not there to restrict us; they free us. In the same way that the Welsh miner's arm was able to move only when it contained a proper scaffolding, external or internal, almost all our movements are made possible because of bone—rigid, inflexible bone.[10]

What Dr. Brand offers as an observation, Jesus stated as a declaration: You will know the truth, and the truth will set you free (John 8:32).

We become free as we build our lives around the framework of God's eternal truth, using its stability and strength to give us freedom.

The world cannot accept this relationship between truth and freedom. Though "always learning," they are "never able to come to the knowledge of the truth" (2 Timothy 3:7 NKJV). Real truth, so the world says, cannot be fixed. It is (if knowable at all), nothing more than a vague sort of intuition that must be adapted to the situation at hand. Any freedom in life is certainly not to be found in the rigid inflexibilities of doctrine and the requirements of an established moral truth. Freedom, to the worldly-minded, means having no limits at all.

But theirs is the freedom of the slug, the earthworm, the formless amoeba. Truth *is* absolute. It is a fixed, stable, never-changing body of moral realities that exists apart from man and his rationalizations. And—just like the marvelous bones in our body that help us move—truth, though rigid, frees us to exercise righteousness, to run in God's path. We become free as we build our lives around the framework of God's eternal truth, using its stability and strength to give us freedom.

The Colossians were hungry for truth. They wanted knowledge and spiritual understanding. But they were being confused by teachers who came into their midst promising a higher form of wisdom and understanding, a "truer" truth than what the Colossians had received in the gospel. Paul wrote to them, warning that they were in danger of being moved away from the real truth and freedom of the gospel, the truth found in Jesus Christ and the freedom that would result in a righteous life. Seventy-six times in his letter he makes reference to Christ. Christ alone, he says, is the image of the invisible God, the Creator and Sustainer of the universe. In Him dwells all the fullness of the Godhead bodily, all the treasures of wisdom and knowledge.

The Colossians needed nothing else but Him.

That message is desperately needed today: *Truth will forever be found in Christ alone.* While the world might rail against Him, angrily declaring the narrowness and exclusivity of His claims, we who believe have found that any limits we encounter in His Word are limits that do nothing but free us to enjoy all that He has for us.

G. K. Chesterton's words ring true: "The more I considered Christianity, the more I found that while it had established a rule and order, the chief aim of that order was to give room for good things to run wild."[11]

Truth. Get to know it. It will set you free!

59

Victory

The Master's Direction

At the early part of the 1800s an artist who was also a great chess player painted a picture of a disturbing game of chess. The two players were a young man and Satan. The young man was given the white pieces and Satan the black. The issue of the game was this: Should the young man win, he was forever free from the power of evil; should the devil win, the young man was to be his slave forever. The artist evidently believed in the supreme power of evil, for his picture portrayed Satan as the victor.

In the conception of the artist, the devil had just moved his queen and had announced a checkmate in four moves. The young man's hand was pictured hovered over his rook; his face paled with fear, for there was no hope. The devil had won! The young man was to be a slave to evil forever.

For many years this picture hung in a great art gallery in Cincinnati, Ohio. Chess players from all over the world came to view the picture. With every conceivable move they tried to help the young man, but to no avail. They hated the work of the artist leaving the devil the winner.

Finally it was concluded that if there was one chess player on earth who could prove the artist wrong, it was the aged Paul Morphy, a resident of New Orleans and the supreme master of chess in his day, an undefeated champion. He had retired sometime earlier from the game due to the mental strain. So a plan was arranged to bring Morphy to Cincinnati to view the picture, and he agreed.

Arriving, he stood before the picture, and two mighty impulses arose in his mind: first, that which leads a brave man to take the role of an underdog; second, that which resents the passing of a crown of supremacy which has not been challenged.

Morphy stood and viewed the painting five minutes, ten minutes, twenty minutes, thirty minutes. He was all concentration; he lifted his hand and lowered it, as in his imagination he made and eliminated moves. Suddenly his hand paused his eyes burned with the vision of a previously unthought-of combination. Then loudly he shouted, "Young man, make that move. That's the move. That's the move!"

To the amazement of all, the old master, the *supreme chess personality,* had discovered a combination that the creating artist had not considered. The way out was there all the time. The young man could defeat the devil. The supreme master had restored hope to all who viewed the picture.

Our lives are much like that of this young man. On our own we have little hope against Satan's powers. But the great assurance is that even when it seems God is silent, our Supreme Master is still there, viewing our lives, waiting for the moment to speak to us His *divine directives,* which always result in victory.

60

Our Heart's Purpose

Some years ago in Shelbyville, Kentucky, Colonel Harland Sanders was sitting on his porch when he received his first Social Security check. "Perhaps it was that moment," he later stated, "that sparked within my heart the determination to launch a new career."

He remembered the delicious fried chicken his mother used to make when he was just a boy. Somehow the aroma seemed to waft across the years, and the recipe he had learned at his mother's apron strings still remained in mind. Then he had a tremendous thought: Why not sell his mother's recipe to restaurant owners? Immediately he began to plan and take action to fulfill his dream. Getting into his car, off he went calling on every restaurant owner he could find. At first no one wanted the recipe of the enthusiastic old gentleman, but finally a Salt Lake City restaurateur gave it a try.

The result was that people thronged the little restaurant for the golden brown chicken the Colonel had cooked. That is where he coined the phrase "It's finger lickin' good."

Finally Colonel Harland Sanders sold his mother's recipe for 2 million dollars, with an additional guarantee of 40,000 dollars each year for the rest of his life. Even today, although he died some years ago, his ruddy face and happy smile are a familiar scene to millions of Americans.

How did he do it? The answer is simple: *He possessed a clear vision and set his heart upon it.* Most of us are very much like the Colonel; we usually do what we set our hearts upon. We follow our visions and our dream. In Proverbs 23:7 we read, "As [a man] thinketh in his heart, so is he" (KJV).

This aptly describes each one of us: Our thoughts, our ideas, and our desires all combine to determine our actions, whether good or bad. Our success in business, in marriage, with our children, and in all other areas of our lives is heavily influenced by what we have determined in our hearts to do or not to do.

If there is correct purpose in the heart, there will be harmony in the soul. If there is harmony in the soul, there will be health in the body. And when there is health in the body, peace in the heart, and harmony in the soul, there is the life that God intended for us to live.

Again in Proverbs we read, "Keep thy heart with all diligence, for out of it are the issues of life" (KJV). Let's be careful what we set our hearts upon!

Notes

1. Michael P. Green, ed., *Illustrations for Biblical Preaching* (Grand Rapids, MI: Baker Book House, 1989), p. 353.

2. Karen Stimer (Colorado Springs, CO: The Masters Group, 1992).

3. Bill Weber, *Conquering the Kill-Joys,* p. 119.

4. Annie Johnson Flint, *1200 Religious Quotations,* Frank S. Mead and Judy G. Mead, eds. (Grand Rapids: Baker Book House, 1965), p. 201.

5. Green, *Illustrations for Biblical Preaching,* pp. 194-95.

6. O.S. Hawkins, *Tracing the Rainbow Through the Rain* (Broadman Press, 1985).

7. Green, *Illustrations for Biblical Preaching,* p. 240.

8. Adapted from Green, *Illustrations for Biblical Preaching,* p. 261.

9. Quoted in Rheta Grimsley Johnson, *Good Grief: The Story of Charles M. Schultz* (New York: Pharos Books, 1989), p. 46. "Peanuts" © 1966, 1976, 1980, 1983, 1985, 1986, 1988, 1989 by United Features Syndicate.

10. Paul Brand and Philip Yancey, *Fearfully and Wonderfully Made* (Grand Rapids, MI: Zondervan, 1987), pp. 81-83.

11. G.K. Chesterton, *Orthodoxy* (Garden City, NY: Doubleday & Co., 1959), p. 95.

Other Good Harvest House Reading

NO GREATER SAVIOR
by *Richard Lee and Ed Hindson*

A collection of 60 brief, powerful meditations that glorify the Lord Jesus Christ and lift readers' to the throne room of God. An invitation to witness our wondrous Savior up close and walk intimately with him.

THERE'S HOPE FOR THE HURTING
by *Richard Lee*

Using illustrations from everyday life as well as examples from the lives of Bible personalities, Dr. Lee reminds us that God will restore and redeem those who cry to Him "out of the depths."

ANGELS OF DECEIT
by *Richard Lee and Ed Hindson*

Why are cults so successful at luring large numbers of followers? Who are the masterminds that make it happen? This book skillfully exposes the strategies used and people behind spiritual deception.

EVERY DAY WITH JESUS
by *Greg Laurie*

Make each day an adventure of spiritual discovery and growth. These brief, powerful meditations, rooted in God's Word and sprinkled with good humor, invite you to take an intimate walk with the Savior.

HIS IMPRINT, MY EXPRESSION
by *Kay Arthur*

An initimate journey for those who long to be shaped by the Master's hand. Wonderfully filled with the promises of Scripture, these devotions focus on Jesus Christ as the answer to every question.

Dear Reader,

We would appreciate hearing from you regarding this Harvest House nonfiction book. It will enable us to continue to give you the best in Christian publishing.

1. What most influenced you to purchase *Windows to the Heart of God?*
   - ❑ Author
   - ❑ Subject matter
   - ❑ Backcover copy
   - ❑ Recommendations
   - ❑ Cover/Title
   - ❑ Other__________

2. Where did you purchase this book?
   - ❑ Christian bookstore
   - ❑ General bookstore
   - ❑ Department store
   - ❑ Grocery store
   - ❑ Other__________

3. Your overall rating of this book?
   ❑ Excellent ❑ Very good ❑ Good ❑ Fair ❑ Poor

4. How likely would you be to purchase other books by this author?
   ❑ Very likely ❑ Not very likely ❑ Somewhat likely ❑ Not at all

5. What types of books most interest you? (Check all that apply.)
   - ❑ Women's Books
   - ❑ Marriage Books
   - ❑ Current Issues
   - ❑ Christian Living
   - ❑ Bible Studies
   - ❑ Fiction
   - ❑ Biographies
   - ❑ Children's Books
   - ❑ Youth Books
   - ❑ Other__________

6. Please check the box next to your age group.
   ❑ Under 18 ❑ 18-24 ❑ 25-34 ❑ 35-44 ❑ 45-54 ❑ 55 and over

Mail to: Editorial Director
Harvest House Publishers
1075 Arrowsmith
Eugene, OR 97402

Name ____

Address ____

State ____________________________ Zip ______________

Thank you for helping us to help you in future publications!